Discovering
WILD PLANT NAMES

John E. Stevens

Illustrations by Molly Hyde

Shire Publications Ltd.

CONTENTS

To my wife

Copyright © 1973 by John E. Stevens. No. 166 in the 'Discovering' series. ISBN 0 85263213 4. First published April 1973. All rights reserved. No part of this publication may be reproduced or transmitted in any form or by any means, electronic or mechanical, including photocopy, recording, or any information storage and retrieval system, without permission in writing from the publishers, Shire Publications Ltd., 12B Temple Square, Aylesbury, Bucks, U.K.

INTRODUCTION

Many plant names are of great antiquity and their original meanings are unknown. Often this is because of grammatical changes, spelling mistakes and wrong words being used during translation from original manuscripts, many of which were written in Greek or Latin. Such errors have been perpetuated and sometimes exaggerated by succeeding writers.

Linnaeus, when arranging his unique classification, used many existing names, as well as inventing them when necessary. For example, in the case of yarrow he chose *Achillea*, a name used for the plant by Dioscorides, as the title for the genus. The species received the name *millefolium* which was another old name that had been used for the plant by herbalists for centuries.

Many common names are derived from early Latin or Old English names and again their antiquity often precludes any certainty as to their original meaning. This book attempts to show some of the suggestions made over the years on the meaning of the names of a limited selection of plants. It is hoped that, if nothing more, these brief notes may add another dimension to a walk through the countryside.

I wish to record my thanks to the Royal Agricultural College and its library for awakening an interest in this subject and for obtaining many books for consultation. My thanks also to Mr D. M. Barling, Mr R. A. Churchill and Mr W. Heatherington of the college Biology Department for their valued advice and encouragement during the compilation of this book. I am particularly indebted to a friend who shall be nameless for much generous advice on etymology and grammar.

Further reading

There are very few books available on this subject but the following would be of interest:

A Gardener's Dictionary of Plant Names; revised by W. T. Stearn; Cassell, 1972.

Englishman's Flora; Geoffrey Grigson; Phoenix, 1960.

Plant Names Simplified; A. T. Johnson and H. A. Smith; Landsmans Bookshop, Bromyard, Hereford, 1972.

If luck is with you your local second-hand bookshop might have a copy of:

Popular Names of British Plants; R. C. A. Prior; Williams & Norgate, 1870.

MEANINGS OF WILD PLANT NAMES

AARON'S ROD (Mullein)   *Verbascum thapsus*
The name 'Aaron's rod' has been given because the tall flowering spike has been compared with descriptions of the staff of
the biblical character. 'Mullein' could have arisen from a number of words: from the French *moleine*, a lung disease of cattle
which the plant was used to treat; or from the Latin *mollis*,
'soft', because of the velvety leaves. Perhaps the best suggestion
is that it is a corruption of *wolleyn* or *wulleyn*, Old English
words meaning 'woollen'. The generic *Verbascum* also is
associated with the hairiness of the plant, for it is probably
derived from the Latin *barba* or *barbascum*, 'bearded'. The
specific *thapsus* refers either to Thapsus, an ancient part of
Africa now called Tunisia, or to the Greek island of Thapsos
where the plant was once common.

AGRIMONY   *Agrimonia eupatoria*
The common and scientific names have the same origin, being
thought to have arisen as a corruption of the Greek *argemos*,
'cataract', an eye disease which some of these plants were supposed to cure. The specific *eupatoria* refers to a fancied similarity between this plant and the hemp agrimony (*Eupatorium
cannabinum*). In fact the two species are very different.

ALDER   *Alnus glutinosa*
The origin of both the common and scientific names is unknown; the former seems to have been 'Aller' in earlier times
but nothing is known of its meaning. The specific *glutinosa*
means 'sticky' and alludes to the leaves, especially whilst still
young.

ALDER BUCKTHORN (Black Dogwood)   *Frangula alnus*
The first name refers to its having been once classified as a
kind of buckthorn with somewhat alder-like leaves; this also
accounts for the use of *alnus* as a specific name. The other
sometimes used name 'black dogwood' is probably occasioned
by the dark-coloured bark, especially when used in contrast
with the true dogwood (*Cornus sp.*) which has reddish branches
and twigs. The generic *Frangula* is derived from the Latin
frangere, 'break', for the branches are very brittle.

APPLE *see* **CRAB APPLE**

4

ASH
Fraxinus excelsior

The origin of the common name is obscure though it may be associated with the Anglo-Saxon *aesc* which came to mean 'spear' as the tree supplied the material for many spear and javelin shafts. A fanciful suggestion links the name with the Norse *Ask*, the name given to the first man who, Scandinavian tradition tells, was created by Odin from an ash tree. The generic *Fraxinus* may be taken from the Greek *phrasso*, 'I fence', or *phraxis*, 'separation', for the tree has traditionally served as both a hedgerow plant and a source of fencing material. The specific *excelsior* means 'taller' or 'loftier'.

ASPARAGUS
Asparagus officinalis

The common and generic name is of very ancient origin and its meaning is obscure. It has been suggested that the name could be linked with the Greek *sparasso*, 'I tear', because of the powerful prickles that some species possess. The specific *officinalis* means 'of the shop'; the plant has long been sold for culinary and medicinal use.

ASPEN
Populus tremula

The common name has unknown origins and nothing can be said other than that it has similar names in many languages of northern Europe. The specific *tremula*, 'trembling', refers to the almost incessant quivering of the leaves, a habit which also accounts for some suggestions on the origin of the generic name *Populus*. This could be taken from the Greek *paipallo*, 'I shake', or perhaps from the Latin *populus*, 'the people', for the Romans used to gather under the trees for their public

Aaron's rod

Basil

meetings, invited there by the chattering leaves. The frequent planting of the trees in Roman towns leads to a suggestion that the name was taken from *arbor-populi*, the 'tree of the people'.

AUTUMN CROCUS *see* MEADOW SAFFRON

BACON AND EGGS *see* BIRD'S-FOOT TREFOIL

BARBERRY *Berberis vulgaris*
The common and generic names are derived from the Arabian name for the plant, *berberys*, which is said to mean 'plant of the Berbers', a people of North Africa. A number of species may be found in this country. The specific *vulgaris* means 'common'.

BARTSIA *see* RED BARTSIA

BASIL *Clinopodium vulgare*
The name 'basil' belongs to a garden herb (*Ocymum*) much used in perfumes and medicines, which explains why it was derived from the Greek *basilikos*, 'royal'. It has a number of similarities to this wild species. The generic *Clinopodium* is taken from the Greek *kline*, 'bed', and *pous*, 'foot'; the flowers have been compared to the castor of a bed-post. The specific *vulgare* simply means 'common'.

BEECH *Fagus sylvatica*
'Beech' as a name is obtained from the Anglo-Saxon *boc* or *bece*, words which by a change in grammatical gender can mean either 'beech tree' or 'book'. The early runic tablets, which could be considered an early form of book, were often carved on beech, and in later times the wood was often used for the covers of the first proper books. The generic *Fagus* is thought to be derived from the Greek *phagein*, 'to eat', because of the edible seeds or mast, whilst the specific *sylvatica* means 'growin woods'.

BEET *Beta vulgaris*
The common and generic names are perhaps derived from the likeness of the twisted form of the fruit to beta, the second letter of the Greek alphabet. The specific *vulgaris* means 'common'.

BELLADONNA *see* DEADLY NIGHTSHADE

BELLBINE (Large Bindweed)   *Calystegia sepium*
The name 'bellbine' refers to the large, bell-shaped flowers and
the climbing, binding habit of growth. This also explains the
other often used common name in which the prefix 'large'
separates it from the similar but smaller species, field bindweed
(*Convolvulus arvensis*). The generic *Calystegia* is thought to be
derived from the Greek *kalyx*, 'cup', and *stege*, 'a covering',
the calyx being often almost hidden by two large bracts (leaf-
like structures).

BETONY   *Betonica officinalis*
According to Pliny the generic and common name originated
as *Vettonica*, a plant of the Vettones, a people of Spain. The
specific *officinalis*, 'of the shop', shows it to have been found
on the premises of the herbalists; it was very much valued in
early medicine.

BILBERRY (Whortleberry)   *Vaccinium myrtillus*
'Bilberry' derives from the Danish *böllebär*, 'dark berry', whilst
'whortleberry' is said to be a corruption of the Latin *myrta* or
myrtillus, old names for a very similar fruit imported during
the Middle Ages and used in medicine and cooking. This also
explains the specific name. The generic *Vaccinium*, a very ancient Latin name is usually unexplained, yet in 1619 Dodoens
in his *New Herbal* made a very logical suggestion that it
could well be a corruption of *baccinium*, this being derived
from the Latin *bacca*, 'berry'.

BINDWEED see **BELLBINE, FIELD BINDWEED**

BIRCH see **SILVER BIRCH**

BIRD'S-FOOT TREFOIL (Bacon and Eggs)
                                                Lotus corniculatus
The arrangement of the fruiting pods has been likened to the
foot of a bird, and the leaf made up of three leaflets explains
the term 'trefoil'. The name 'bacon and eggs' refers to the
colour of the flowers, some being just yellow and others tinged
with red. The meaning of the generic *Lotus* is unknown; it is
taken from the classical Greek *lotos*, a name applied to a wide
variety of plants. The specific *corniculatus*, 'bearing small
horns', is a further reference to the form of the fruiting
pods.

BIRD'S-NEST ORCHID   *Neottia nidus-avis*
The common and scientific names almost all refer to the tangled

and matted root system being likened to a bird's nest. In Greek *neottia* means 'bird's nest' as does the Latin *nidus-avis*. The term 'orchid' is taken from the Greek *orchis* meaning 'testicle', an allusion to the double tubers of many members of the family.

BISHOPWEED *see* GOUTWEED

BISTORT (Easter Ledges, Snake Root)   *Polygonum bistorta*
The names 'bistort', 'snake root' and the specific *bistorta*, which means 'twice-turned', all refer to the twisted root system. 'Easter ledges' originated from an early name for the plant, *aristolochia*, which was corrupted into 'Astrologia' and then, as the plant was sometimes eaten at Easter, it became 'Easter-logia' and eventually 'Easter ledges'. *Aristolochia* is derived from Greek words meaning 'best childbirth'; it is possible the plant was used in this event because of its strong astringent properties (the name is now used for the birthwort). The generic name is taken from the Greek *polys*, 'many', and *gony*, 'knee'; it refers to the swollen joints on the stems of many species.

BITTERSWEET (Woody Nightshade)   *Solanum dulcamara*
'Bittersweet' and the specific *dulcamara*, which means the same, have been used because parts of the plant if tasted are at first bitter and then produce a sweet sensation. 'Woody nightshade' indicates that the plant is a woody perennial, in contrast to the closely related herbaceous perennial, the black nightshade (*S. nigrum*). The term 'nightshade' seems to have arisen when an early medical name *solatrum* was mistaken for *solem atrum*, 'black sun' or 'shade as of night'. The generic *Solanum* was given to one of the nightshades by Pliny and could be derived from the Latin *solamen*, 'solace', or *solor*, 'comfort', because of the narcotic effects of some species. Another possibility is that the name could be associated with the Latin *sol*, 'the sun', because of the shape of the flowers. A final suggestion is that the name should have been *sulanum*, this being derived from the Latin *sus*, 'swine', as some species were used to treat certain pig disorders.

BLACK BRYONY   *Tamus communis*
The common name refers to the dark green leaves and black root as compared with the paler leaves and root of the white bryony (*Bryonia dioica*). The term 'bryony' is derived from the Greek *bryo*, 'I sprout', an allusion to the rapid growth of the stems. The generic name *Tamus* was given by Columella to a

Bistort

Bittersweet

vine-like plant; it was used by Linnaeus because this plant has a similar habit of growth. The specific *communis* means 'common' or 'growing in company'.

BLACK MEDICK   *Medicago lupulina*

The common and the generic name originated in *medike*, a name given by Dioscorides to some species from Media (Persia), the country where lucerne is said to have been first grown. The prefix 'black' refers to the colour of the seed pods. The specific *lupulina* means 'hop-like', probably because of a fancied similarity in flower shape.

BLACKTHORN (Sloe)   *Prunus spinosa*

The thorny nature of the plant combined with the dark-coloured bark explains one of the common names and the specific *spinosa*, which means 'bearing spines'. 'Sloe' is derived from the Anglo-Saxon *sla* or *slag*, words that are closely allied to a verb meaning 'to strike', perhaps being so used because the wood was once used in making flails and bludgeons. The generic *Prunus* is an ancient Classical name for the plum, and is of unknown meaning.

BLUE BUTCHER *see* EARLY PURPLE ORCHID

BLUEBELL (Wild Hyacinth)   *Endymion non-scriptus*

'Bluebell' is a reference to the blue, bell-shaped flowers, whilst the name 'hyacinth' originates from early workers who classified the plant as a hyacinth (named after a Greek youth, Hyakinthos, who was accidentally killed by Apollo). The specific *non-scriptus*, 'without marking', probably refers to some of the early hyacinths having marks on their petals; another reason could be that this plant was overlooked by the Greeks and Romans; William Turner seems to have been the first to describe it in 1548. The generic name *Endymion* is also connected with mythology, for it honours a Greek youth of that name who was doomed to everlasting sleep on Mount Latmos. For the Bluebell of Scotland, see Harebell.

BOG ASPHODEL   *Narthecium ossifragum*
The common name of this marsh plant means 'bog lily'; the term 'asphodel' belongs to a stately plant of great beauty (Greek *a*, 'without', and *sphallo*, 'I surpass'). The generic name is said to be taken from the Greek *narthex*, a plant with pithy stalks, and is a reference to the hollow stems. The specific *ossifragum* means 'bone-breaking', from an old belief that the bones of sheep who eat it will become brittle and easily fractured.

BOGBEAN (Buckbean)   *Menyanthes trifoliata*
The similarity in foliage of this marsh plant to that of the bean accounts for the common names, and the specific *trifoliata* means 'three-leaved'. The term 'buck' was probably taken from the French *bouc* meaning 'male goat'; an early name for the plant was goat's bean. The generic *Menyanthes* derives from the Greek *men*, 'month', and *anthos*, 'flower', either because it was said to last for one month, or because it was once used medicinally to bring on menstruation. It could also have been simply borrowed from the name 'moonflower', used for one of the water-lilies.

BOX   *Buxus sempervirens*
The common and generic names are of extremely ancient origin, perhaps deriving from the Greek *pyknos*, 'dense', because of either the hard, close-grained wood or the foliage which excludes almost all light. The specific *sempervirens* means 'evergreen'.

BRANDY BOTTLE *see* YELLOW WATER-LILY

BROOKLIME   *Veronica beccabunga*
The common name refers to its place of growth; it was called by some old writers 'broke lympe'. The generic *Veronica* is of obscure meaning; it could be a corruption of *Betonica* (betony) because of similarities in leaf shape. The markings on the flowers of some species have been thought to be like those

Black medick   *Brooklime*

found on the handkerchief of St. Veronica after being used to wipe the face of Jesus as he carried his cross. A final suggestion is that it comes from the Arabic *viroo nikoo*, 'beautiful memory', from the pretty flowers. The specific *beccabunga* is thought to be derived from the old German (1640) *bachpunghen*, 'mouth smart', in reference to its acrid taste.

BROOM   *Sarothamnus scoparius*
The name 'broom' simply refers to early use of the twigs for sweeping. So does the generic name, being derived from the Greek *saron*, 'besom', and *thamnos*, 'shrub'. The specific *scoparius* also means 'brush-' or 'broom-like'.

BROOMRAPE *see* GREATER BROOMRAPE

BRYONY *see* BLACK BRYONY, WHITE BRYONY

BUCKBEAN *see* BOGBEAN

BUCKTHORN   *Rhamnus catharticus*
It is possible that during early translations the German *buxdorn* meaning 'box-thorn' was mistaken for *bocksdorn*, 'buck's thorn'; both these plants are strong purgatives and such use helped emphasise the confusion. The generic *Rhamnus* is probably taken from the Greek *rhamnos*, a name for some thorny shrub. The specific *catharticus* is a further reference to its purgative qualities. See also Alder Buckthorn.

BUGLE
Ajuga reptans

The origins of the name 'bugle' are obscure. The flowers are vaguely trumpet-shaped and the leaves have been likened to tube-shaped glass beads, called bugles, once sewn upon clothing. Pliny used the name *abuga* for some similar plant, so the common name could be a corruption of this, as also could the generic name. This latter name could also be derived from the Greek *a*, 'without', and *zygon*, 'a yoke', because the lobes of the calyx are equal. The specific *reptans* means 'creeping'; the plant is stoloniferous.

BUGLOSS *see* VIPER'S BUGLOSS

BUSH VETCH
Vicia sepium

The common name 'vetch' and generic *Vicia* are thought to derive from the Latin *vincio*, 'I bind', because of the tendrils that many species possess. The common name thus speaks of a climbing, binding plant that forms dense, almost bushy clumps. The specific *sepium* means 'of hedgerows'.

BUTTERCUP *see* CREEPING BUTTERCUP

BUTTERWORT
Pinguicula vulgaris

The common name alludes to the greasy-looking leaves which seem to have had butter poured over them, an appearance reflected in the generic name, for this is derived from the Latin *pinguis* meaning 'fat'. The specific *vulgaris* means 'common'.

CABBAGE
Brassica oleracea

'Cabbage' is probably derived from the French *caboche* meaning 'head' in reference to the large swollen apical stem buds that are cut for eating. The specific *oleracea* means 'eatable'. The generic *Brassica* is of great antiquity and its original meaning is unknown; it was used for the cabbage by Pliny.

CAMPION *see* RED CAMPION

CARLINE THISTLE
Carlina vulgaris

The common and generic names are taken from Charles the Great, the Emperor Charlemagne. He prayed to God when his men were dying of disease; an angel appeared, fired an arrow in the air and told the emperor to mark the plant upon which it fell, for it would cure the pestilence. It fell upon the carline thistle. The term 'thistle' reached us from the Anglo-Saxon *thistel* but its meaning is unknown. The specific *vulgaris* means 'common'.

CARROT
Daucus carota

The common and specific names have the same origin deriving from its Greek name *karoton* which is perhaps linked with the red colour of the root. The generic *Daucus*, another old Greek name of obscure origin, has been suggested to derive from *daio* meaning 'I make hot' or 'burn' in reference to some supposed medical quality.

CAT MINT
Nepeta cataria

An old belief was that cats love this plant and if they eat or smell it they become 'frolicsome, loving and full of fight'. For this reason the common name and specific *cataria* meaning 'of cats' have been applied. The generic *Nepeta* is said to be taken from Nepet, a town in Tuscany where the plants were first noted. The plant is somewhat similar to the Mints (*Mentha* sp.) and the origin of this name will be considered under Pennyroyal.

CELANDINE *see* LESSER CELANDINE, GREATER CELANDINE

CHESTNUT *see* HORSE CHESTNUT, SWEET CHESTNUT

CHICORY (Succory)
Cichorium intybus

The common and generic names probably both derive from the Arabic name of one of these plants, *chicouryeh*. The specific *intybus* is Latin for 'endive', which is an old name for this plant. 'Succory' is probably a corruption of 'chicory' and is now usually applied to the salad plant endive which has been given

Broom

Carline thistle

its own specific status. The meaning of the early names is un-known.

CLEAVERS (Goosegrass) *Galium aparine*

'Cleave' meaning 'stick' or 'adhere' is a word that has almost passed from our language and is now perpetuated mostly by the name of this plant. How tenaciously the seeds stick to clothing! The specific *aparine* meaning 'clinging' also refers to this and to its scrambling habit of growth. 'Goosegrass' alludes to early beliefs that geese cured themselves of disease by eating it; goslings are particularly fond of it. The generic *Galium* is taken from the Greek *gala*, 'milk', and refers to some species being once used for curdling milk.

CLOVER *see* RED CLOVER

CODLINS AND CREAM (Great Hairy Willowherb)
Epilobium hirsutum

The name 'codlins and cream' has been applied because the bruised plant has a smell reminiscent of boiled apples. The name 'willowherb', first used by Lyte in 1578, refers to a simi-larity in leaf shape between this plant and the willow. A tall plant with hairy stems, it is called the great hairy willowherb to distinguish it from smaller non-hairy species. The specific *hirsutum* also means 'hairy'. The generic *Epilobium* derives from the Greek *epi*, 'upon', and *lobos*, 'a pod'—the flowers appear to be at the end of the fruiting pod.

Cleavers   *Codlins and cream*

COLTSFOOT
Tussilago farfara

The shape of the leaves being likened to an animal's foot explains the name 'coltsfoot'. The generic *Tussilago* is taken from the Latin *tussis*, 'cough'; from time immemorial the plant has been used in the treatment of pulmonary complaints. The specific *farfara*, an extremely ancient name, apparently originated because the leaves were compared with those of the white poplar; *farfara* derives from a Greek name for this tree.

COMFREY
Symphytum officinale

Comfrey is derived either from the Latin *confirmo*, 'I strengthen', or *confero*, 'I gather together', and refers to early uses in the treatment of fractures. The plant was given many uses in medicine which explains the scientific name, for *Symphytum* is thought to be from the Greek *symphyo*, 'I make whole', and *phyton*, 'plant', whilst the specific *officinale*, meaning 'of the shop', shows it could have been obtained from the herbalist's premises.

CORN GROMWELL
Lithospermum arvense

The plant has very hard fruits, which explains the generic name derived from the Greek *lithos*, 'stone', and *sperma*, 'seed'. The herbalists called the gromwell (*L. officinale*) *granum solis*, 'grain of the sun', and *milium solis*, 'millet of the sun'; it is thought that these words were eventually combined (*granum* and *milium*) producing the medieval Latin *gruinum milium*, 'crane's millet', from which the word 'gromwell' derives. This species is a plant of arable fields as indicated by the prefix 'corn' in the common name and *arvense* in the scientific name, which means 'growing in fields'.

Coltsfoot

Cow parsnip

CORNBINE *see* FIELD BINDWEED

COW PARSNIP (Hogweed) *Heracleum sphondylium*
Both common names probably mean it is a worthless parsnip,
fit only for pigs and cattle. The generic *Heracleum* is said to
honour the Greek hero, Hercules, who discovered its medicinal virtues. The specific *sphondylium* is a very ancient name
for the plant which seems, like its Italian name *spondilo*, to be
derived from a Greek word meaning 'vertebra', possibly because of the hollow internodes of the stems.

COWSLIP *Primula veris*
The common name has very obscure origins. The wrinkled texture of the leaves has been likened to a cow's lip and to a pre-
paration of a calf's stomach used as rennet in Yorkshire and
called keslop. It has also been suggested as deriving from cow-
slop or cow-pat, it being said that the plant is especially common where dung has fallen. The scientific name refers to its
early flowering, for *Primula* derives from the Latin *primus*,
'first', and the specific *veris* means 'of the spring'.

COW WHEAT *Melampyrum pratense*
The generic name derives from the Greek *melas*, 'black', and
pyros, 'wheat', a reference to the seed which is about the size
of a wheat grain and, when ground and mixed with flour, will
turn it black. Hence, too, the common name, with the prefix
'cow' applied because cattle were said to be very fond of it and,
according to Linnaeus, produce the yellowest butter where this
species abounds. The specific *pratense* means 'growing in
meadows', not very appropriate for a plant more typical of
woods and heaths.

CRAB APPLE *Malus sylvestris*
The common name is derived from the Anglo-Saxon *scrobb*,
'shrub', hence the term 'crab', but the word 'apple' is of unknown meaning. The generic *Malus*, an old Latin name for the
apple, is also of obscure meaning, but might be derived from
the Greek *malakos*, 'soft', owing to the edible fruit. The specific *sylvestris* means 'wild'.

CREEPING BUTTERCUP *Ranunculus repens*
It was once believed that pastures containing many buttercups
would produce butter of a very good colour. 'Cup' could well
refer to the yellow cup-like flower but is perhaps more likely to
be a relic of the Anglo-Saxon *cop* meaning 'head'. The plant is
stoloniferous which explains the use of the prefix 'creeping' and

the specific *repens*, which means the same. The generic *Ranunculus* derives from the Latin *rana*, 'a frog', because many species inhabit moist places.

CUCKOO FLOWER (Lady's Smock)   *Cardamine pratensis*

'Cuckoo flower' is a name probably applied because the plant flowers around the time that the cuckoo is first heard. 'Lady's smock' is a name given to the plant because of a fancied resemblance of the pale lilac flowers to little smocks hanging out to dry. The generic *Cardamine* is taken from the Greek name for watercress, *kardamon*, on account of its similar taste; this latter species was once used as a heart sedative and its name derives from the Greek *kardia*, 'heart', and *damao*, 'subdue'. The specific *pratensis* means 'growing in meadows'.

CUCKOO PINT (Lords and Ladies)   *Arum maculatum*

The name 'cuckoo pint' arose from the Anglo-Saxon *cucu* meaning 'lively' and *pintle*, 'a vertical projecting pin', a reference to the shape of the spiked flower. The name is often thought to imply the male organ of reproduction, which is why many Victorian books chose to ignore it. The other often used name, 'lords and ladies', is a children's name for the plant; the club-shaped inflorescence can be purple or white; the purple were called 'lords' and the white, 'ladies'. The generic *Arum* derives from the Greek *aron*, a name for some poisonous plants, whilst the specific *maculatum* means 'spotted' and refers to the leaves, which are often blotched.

Cuckoo pint   *Daffodil*

DAFFODIL
Narcissus pseudo-narcissus

'Daffodil' originated in the Greek *asphodelus* (see Bog Aspho-del), a plant that grew in the meadows of Persephone, Queen of Hades, and for some unknown reason the early writers gave the name to this plant; over the years it became corrupted to its present form. The generic *Narcissus* is an ancient Classical name from Greece. Mythology tells that Narcissus was a youth who was overcome and died from the force of the love he felt for his own reflection; the earth sent forth the flower that bears his name in memory. The specific *pseudo-narcissus* means 'false-narcissus' and was probably given to separate it from the narcissus of the poets (*N. poeticus*) which is sometimes called the 'true narcissus', and is the one that has the legendary origin.

DAISY
Bellis perennis

'Daisy' is taken from the Anglo-Saxon *dæges-eage* meaning 'eye of day', as it opens and closes its flowers with daylight. The generic *Bellis* is probably taken from the Latin *bella*, 'pretty', though the plant's power as a wound herb makes it possible that the name is associated with the Latin *bellum*, 'war'. Mythology tells that it is named after the Belides, one of whom died in fear of Vertumnus, god of Spring, sinking to the earth in the form of a daisy. The specific *perennis* means 'perennial'.

DANDELION
Taraxacum officinale

The common name 'dandelion' derives from the French *dent de lion* meaning 'lion's tooth', perhaps in allusion to the jagged leaves. Another reason could be the great medicinal virtues of the plant which allow it to be likened to the tooth of a lion, which was also reputed to possess great curative properties. These uses also explain the specific *officinale* as it would cer-tainly have been found on the premises of the early herbalists. The generic *Taraxacum* is of very ancient origin, probably de-riving from an Arabic name *talkh chakok* meaning 'bitter plant'.

DEADLY NIGHTSHADE (Dwale, Belladonna)
Atropa belladonna

The term 'nightshade' has been considered previously (see Bittersweet) with the prefix 'deadly' referring to its very pois-onous properties. 'Dwale' is a Scandinavian term for some-thing that dulls the senses and causes sleep, and alludes to the narcotic powers of this plant. The word 'belladonna', used both as a common and specific name, is a very ancient title for the

18

Dandelion   *Deadly nightshade*

plant and means 'fair lady'; apparently the Roman ladies used the juice for dilating the pupils of the eyes, a cosmetic practice that was then thought desirable. The generic *Atropa* is another reference to the toxicity of the plant, from the Greek Atropos, one of the Fates whose duty was to cut the threads of human life.

DEADNETTLE *see* WHITE DEADNETTLE

DEVIL'S BIT SCABIOUS   *Succisa pratensis*
This plant has an abruptly shortened root that looks almost as if it has been bitten off. It is said that the plant used to have a quite long root that could be used for curing almost all diseases and that the devil, grudging man such a useful medicine, took a bite from it. 'Scabious' derives from the Latin *scabies* 'itch'; some related species having been once used to treat a number of skin diseases. The generic name also refers to the shortened root, being derived from the Latin *succisum* meaning 'broken off'; the specific *pratensis* means 'of meadows'.

DODDER   *Cuscuta epithymum*
The common name may have its origin in the Frisian *dodd*, 'bunch', or Dutch *dot*, 'tangled thread', in allusion to the tangled mass of thread-like stems this parasitic plant forms over its host species. The generic *Cuscuta* is an ancient name of unknown meaning, possibly deriving from its Arabic name *kechout*. The specific *epithymum* means 'upon thyme' as it was once thought to be restricted to thyme as a host plant; certainly it is often found on this plant, but also on a wide range of other species.

DOG ROSE   *Rosa canina*
The prefix 'dog' in the common name and the specific *canina*,
'pertaining to a dog', have been applied either as simply meaning a wild rose of little merit or perhaps in allusion to an early
medicinal use in treating people bitten by a mad dog. The
generic name *Rosa* from which the common name derives is a
Latin name whose meaning is unknown.

DOG'S MERCURY   *Mercurialis perennis*
The common and generic names are traditionally supposed to
honour the god Mercury who, according to Pliny, first discovered it. The prefix 'dog' is used in a derogatory sense and indicates worthlessness. The plant is a perennial as shown by the
specific *perennis*, used to distinguish the plant from the closely
related annual mercury (*M. annua*).

DROPWORT   *Filipendula vulgaris*
The common name refers to the root system which has a number of small tubers on slender thread-like roots. This also explains the generic name, which is derived from the Latin *filum*,
'thread', and *pendulus*, 'hanging'. The specific *vulgaris* means
'common', a little confusing because it is not the most fre-
quently seen member of the genus in the British Isles; meadow-
sweet (*F. ulmaria*) is much more common.

DWALE *see* DEADLY NIGHTSHADE

DYER'S GREENWEED   *Genista tinctoria*
The specific *tinctoria*, 'of dyers', was applied because the plant
was a source of yellow dye which could be made into green by
mixing it with the blue obtained from woad—hence the common name. The generic *Genista*, broom, is Latin and of unknown meaning.

EARLY PURPLE ORCHID (Blue Butcher)   *Orchis mascula*
The first common name refers to early flowering and purplish
flowers. 'Blue butcher' probably originated as 'bloody butcher'
as the dark blotches on the leaves resemble blood spots. The
generic *Orchis* and common name 'orchid', are derived from
the Greek *orchis*, 'testicle', an allusion to the double tubers of
many species. The specific *mascula* means 'male'; the early
writers often called vigorous, red-flowered plants male to separate them from more delicate blue-flowered ones which they
considered feminine.

Devil's bit scabious   *Dog rose*

EARTHNUT (Pignut)   *Conopodium majus*

The plant has a large tuberous root said to be nut-like in flavour and eagerly rooted out by pigs. The generic *Conopodium* derives from the Greek *konos*, 'cone', and *pous*, 'foot', and is a reference to the shape of the flowers with their inwardly turned tips. *Majus* means 'larger'.

EASTER LEDGES *see* BISTORT

ELDER   *Sambucus nigra*

Elder is a name probably derived from the Anglo-Saxon *aeld* meaning 'kindle', either from the pith having been used to start fires or from the hollow stems being used to blow the glowing tinder into a flame. The generic *Sambucus*, another ancient name, could be associated with the Latin *sambuca*, a 'harp' made from the wood of some species. *Nigra* means 'black', the colour of the ripe fruit.

ENCHANTER'S NIGHTSHADE   *Circaea lutetiana*

The common and generic names honour the enchantress Circe because the hooked spines on the fruits catch the clothes of passing folk as closely as Circe would have done with her spells. The name also belonged to the mandrake, which was once classed as a 'nightshade' and also much used in magic; it seems that the two names became erroneously mixed. The specific *lutetiana* means 'of Paris', a city whose ancient name was Lutetia.

EVERGREEN OAK (Holm Oak, Ilex)   *Quercus ilex*

The tree is not deciduous like the normal oak but is very similar in other respects and bears acorns. The other common names arise from the likening of the leaves to those of holly, and are a little confusing for whilst 'holm' is an early name for holly, derived from its Anglo-Saxon name *holen*, 'ilex', a very old name for this tree, is used as the generic name for holly. These names therefore really mean 'holly-like oak'. The generic *Quercus* is discussed under 'Oak'.

EYEBRIGHT   *Euphrasia officinalis*

The plant was used in early times as a cure for many diseases of the eyes, hence the common name and specific *officinalis*. The generic *Euphrasia* derives from the Greek *euphrasio*, 'delight', and was probably applied because of the plant's use in curing blindness.

FAIRY FLAX (Purging Flax)   *Linum catharticum*

The plant is very much a tiny copy of the cultivated flax, hence the use of the prefix 'fairy'. The medicinal use in the past as a purgative explains the other common name and specific *catharticum*. The generic *Linum*, flax, is a very ancient name whose derivation is unknown.

FAT HEN   *Chenopodium album*

The common name seems to have been applied from an early belief that the plant was good for fattening poultry, or perhaps because it often appears in chicken runs after the birds have been removed. The generic *Chenopodium* derives from the Greek *chen*, 'goose', and *pous*, 'foot', because of the shape of the leaves of some species. The specific *album*, 'white', is a reference to the light-coloured leaves.

FIELD BINDWEED (Cornbine)   *Convolvulus arvensis*

The meanings of the common names of this scrambling, binding plant are obvious and echoed by the generic name, taken from the Latin *convolvo*, 'I intertwine'. The specific *arvensis* means 'growing in fields'.

FIELD MADDER   *Sherardia arvensis*

The common name is owed to similarities between this plant and the true madder (*Rubia tinctorum*) and to its habitat, as does the specific *arvensis*, 'growing in fields'. The name 'madder' derives from the Low German *made*, 'worm', and was applied from a confusion between the red dye made from the root of the plant and another red colour, made from insects that infest a species of oak (*Quercus coccifera*); in early days many insects were called 'worms'. The generic *Sherardia* honours an early patron of botany, William Sherard (1659–1728).

FIELD POPPY *Papaver rhoeas*

The common name comes from the Anglo-Saxon *papig* but no more is known of its meaning nor of the origin of the generic *Papaver*. The specific *rhoeas* seems to mean 'flowing' and probably describes how easily the seed flows from the ripe capsules or the petals fall when picked.

FIELD SCABIOUS *Knautia arvensis*

This is a plant of grassy places, hence the use of 'field' in the common name and the specific *arvensis*, 'growing in fields'. The term 'scabious' derives from the Latin *scabies* meaning 'itch'; some of these plants were once used in treating leprosy and other skin diseases. The generic name honours Dr C. Knaut, a German physician and botanical writer from Halle in Saxony, who died in 1694.

FIGWORT *Scrophularia nodosa*

The specific *nodosa* means 'knotty', a reference to the short, nodular rhizomes which were once used in treating scrophulous swellings—hence the generic name. The plant was also used to treat a disease called *ficus*, this being the Latin name for the fig, which explains the origin of the common name.

FIREWEED *see* ROSEBAY WILLOWHERB

Dyer's greenweed

Eyebright

FOOL'S PARSLEY
Aethusa cynapium

The common name refers to its being a somewhat parsley-like plant that only a fool would mistake, or that it would be dangerous to mistake, for it is poisonous. The generic name is thought to derive from the Greek *aithusso*, 'I kindle', owing to its powerful toxic properties. The specific *cynapium* comes from the Greek *kyon*, 'dog', and *apium*, the name of some similar plant, and means 'worthless parsley'.

FORGET-ME-NOT
Myosotis arvensis

The common name first belonged to the ground pine because of the nauseous taste it left in the mouth; early in the nineteenth century for some unknown reason it became transferred to this genus. The generic *Myosotis* derives from the Greek *mys*, 'mouse', and *ous*, 'ear', in allusion to the shape and texture of the leaves. *Arvensis* is 'growing in fields'.

FOXGLOVE
Digitalis purpurea

The common name was applied in very early times. It could be taken from the Anglo-Saxon *foxes-glew*, 'fox-music', because of the bell-shaped flowers. A charming country tale tells that the bad fairies gave the plant to the fox so that he could put flowers on his toes and prowl the chicken roosts in silence. The generic name was given by Fuchs in 1542 and is taken from the Latin *digitus*, 'finger', in reference to the flowers being likened to the fingers of a glove. The specific *purpurea* means 'purple', the usual colour of the flowers.

FRITILLARY (Snake's Head)
Fritillaria melaegris

The common name 'fritillary' and generic *Fritillaria* derive from the Latin *fritillus*, 'dice-box', because the markings on the petals can be likened to those of a chequer board. Similarly the specific *melaegris* means 'speckled'; it is the Greek name for a Guinea hen. The name 'snake's head' describes the shape of the flower bud.

FURZE *see* GORSE

GALLANT SOLDIER
Galingsoga parviflora

The common name is a straight corruption of the generic name which honours a Spanish botanist, Don Mariano de Galingsoga, once superintendent of the Madrid botanic gardens. The specific *parviflora* means 'small-flowered'.

GENTIAN *see* MARSH GENTIAN

Fat hen   *Fritillary*

GIPSYWORT   *Lycopus europaeus*
This plant yields a dark-coloured dye and it has been said that gipsies used it to darken their complexions. The generic name is derived from the Greek *lykos*, 'wolf', and *pous*, 'foot', because of the shape of the leaves. The specific *europaeus* means 'of Europe'.

GLOBE FLOWER   *Trollius europaeus*
The flower is globe-shaped and the generic *Trollius* is thought to be taken from the Old German *trol* meaning 'something round'. The specific *europaeus* means 'of Europe'.

GOAT'S BEARD (Jack-go-to-bed-at-noon)
                 Tragopogon pratensis
The large feathery hairs on the seed account for the common and generic names; the latter derives from the Greek *tragos*, 'goat', and *pogon*, 'beard'. The alternative common name arose because the flowers are always closed by mid-day. The specific *pratensis* means 'growing in meadows'.

GOOSEGRASS *see* **CLEAVERS**

GORSE (Furze)   *Ulex europaeus*
'Gorse' probably comes from the Anglo-Saxon *gorst*, 'a waste', the plant often growing in rough places. The other often used name, 'furze', is thought to come from the Anglo-Saxon *fyrs* —the plant was once commonly used as firewood. *Ulex*, an ancient name used by Pliny for some spiny shrub, is of unknown meaning. The specific name means 'of Europe'.

GOUTWEED (Bishopweed, Ground Elder)
Aegopodium podagraria

The plant was once used in the treatment of gout, an affliction traditionally said to attack senior clergymen—hence a possible explanation of 'bishopweed'. However, another explanation is that it was given to those who did not regularly attend church, as a reminder of their sins. The name 'ground elder' was given because the plant has elder-like leaves and creeps through the soil. *Aegopodium* derives from the Greek *aix*, 'goat', and *pous*, 'foot', from some fancied resemblance of leaf shape. The specific *podagraria*, meaning 'gout', again refers to its medicinal use.

GREATER BROOMRAPE
Orobanche rapum-genistae

This parasite attaches itself to the roots of such plants as gorse and broom. It has a swollen base to its stem and the Latin *rapa* means 'turnip'. This species is quite large in comparison with others. The generic *Orobanche*, derived from the Greek *orobos* 'vetch' and *ancho*, 'I strangle', springs from its parasitic habit. The specific name means 'broom-rape', the old name for broom being *Genista*.

GREATER CELANDINE
Chelidonium majus

The common and generic names are both derived from *chelidon*, the Greek for the swallow, perhaps because of an old belief that the plant flowers and fades with the arrival and departure of the bird. Another old story claims that the swallow uses the plant to heal and restore the sight of its young. The specific *majus* means 'larger'; this and the prefix 'greater' in the common name differentiate the plant from the totally unrelated but similarly named lesser celandine (*Ranunculus ficaria*).

GROMWELL *see* CORN GROMWELL

GROUND ELDER *see* GOUTWEED

GROUND IVY
Glechoma hederacea

The common name has been applied because it is a plant with somewhat ivy-like leaves that runs along the ground, and the specific *hederacea* also means 'ivy-like'. The generic *Glechoma* derives from the Greek *glechon*, 'mint' or 'thyme'; the early workers did not make a clear distinction between these plants.

GROUNDSEL
Senecio vulgaris

The name 'groundsel' originated in the Anglo-Saxon *grundswelge* meaning 'ground glutton', probably because vast numbers of these plants can appear very suddenly. The generic *Senecio* is taken from the Latin *senex*, 'old', probably because of the white and hoary seed hairs. Another suggestion is that the naked receptacle, after the seeds have gone, can be likened to a bald head. The specific *vulgaris* means 'common'.

GUELDER ROSE   *Viburnum opulus*
The common name refers to the somewhat rose-like balls of white flowers and to Gueldres or Guelderland, a region on the border of Holland and Germany, once thought to be its native country and where varieties were often cultivated. The name *Viburnum* is of very ancient origin, perhaps deriving from the Latin *vieo*, 'tie', the pliable branches of some species having been used as a binding material. The specific *opulus* is probably associated with the Latin *opulens*, 'rich', referring to the showy red berries, which contrast with the black ones of the closely related wayfaring tree. It has also been suggested that it might also be a mis-spelling of *populus*, there being some similarity between the leaves of this tree and those of the white poplar.

HARDHEADS *see* KNAPWEED

HAREBELL (Bluebell of Scotland)   *Campanula rotundifolia*
'Harebell' could have been so called because it is found in grassy places where hares can often be seen. Another possibility is that it should really be 'hairbell', referring to the bell-shaped flower on its thin, hair-like stalk. It is obvious why the plant should be called bluebell but not why this name should only have been commonly used in Scotland. The generic *Campanula* is the Latin for 'a small bell'. The specific *rotundifolia* means 'round-leaved', not obvious unless the basal leaves can be seen, and these may have withered away by the time the plant blooms.

HAWKBIT   *Leontodon autumnalis*
The common name was given because of an old belief that hawks use these plants to strengthen their eyesight. *Leontodon* derives from the Greek for 'lion' and 'tooth'—the leaves have jagged, tooth-like divisions. The specific name refers to the plant's usual time of flowering.

HAWKWEED *see* MOUSE-EAR HAWKWEED

HAWTHORN   *Crataegus monogyna*
The common name really means 'hedge-thorn' for 'haw' has the

27

same derivation as the Anglo-Saxon *harga* or *hoege,* 'hedge-row'. The generic *Crataegus* derives from the Greek *kratos,* 'strength', and the hardness of the wood. The plant usually has only one style (the structure connecting ovary to stigma) hence the use of the specific *monogyna.* There is a closely related Midland hawthorn which usually has two styles.

HAZEL   *Corylus avellana*
The common name may be derived from the Anglo-Saxon *haesel* meaning 'command'; hazel sticks have long been used in enforcing orders, both to cattle and slaves. The generic *Corylus* is thought to derive from the Greek *korys,* 'helmet', from the way the calyx almost covers the nut. The specific *avellana* refers to Avella, a town near Naples, where the plant was grown for its fruit.

HEATHER (Ling)   *Calluna vulgaris*
The name 'heather' is of very obscure origin whilst 'ling' possibly derives from *lig,* the Anglo-Saxon for 'fire', the plant having been used as a fuel. It was also used as a broom, hence *Calluna,* derived from the Greek *kallyno,* 'I cleanse'. The specific *vulgaris* means 'common'.

HEMLOCK   *Conium maculatum*
The common name is thought to be taken from the Anglo-Saxon *hoem* or *healm,* 'straw', and *leac,* 'plant', a reference to the dry, hollow stalks that remain after flowering. *Conium* is possibly derived from the Greek *konis,* 'powder', the powdered plant having been used by the ancient Greeks as a poison. The specific *maculatum* means 'spotted', and refers to the characteristic purple blotches on the stems.

HEMP AGRIMONY   *Eupatorium cannabinum*
In early days the plant was classed with the quite different agrimony and this, and its somewhat hemp-like leaves, accounts for the common name. The generic name honours Mithridates Eupator, king of Pontus, who first discovered the value of a similar plant as a counter poison. The specific *cannabinum* means 'hemp-like', this plant resembling hemp (*Cannabis sativa*).

HENBANE   *Hyoscyamus niger*
'Henbane' is a name applied from an early belief that hens who had eaten the seeds would soon die. It seems, however, that it was not fatal to all animals, for it has been suggested that the generic *Hyoscyamus* derives from the Greek *hys,* 'hog', and

kyamos, 'bean', because the fruits were much favoured by swine. The specific *niger* means 'black' and probably alludes to the plant's poisonous narcotic qualities or, alternatively, to an old belief that any part of the body to which it was applied would turn black and rot.

HERB PARIS   *Paris quadrifolia*
The generic name is derived from the Latin *par* meaning 'equal', referring to the regularity of the flower parts and leaves, which are usually in fours. Hence also *quadrifolia*, which means 'four-leaved'. The common name derives from an early Latin title, *herba paris*, 'herb of equality'.

HERB ROBERT   *Geranium robertianum*
The use of 'Robert' in the common and specific names has very obscure origins. It could honour St. Robert, founder of the Cistercian Order, who was born on 29th April, the time the plant is usually beginning to flower. Another possibility is that it is a corruption of an old name 'rubwort'; it has even been suggested that it commemorates the virtues of Robin Hood. Perhaps the most likely reason is that it derives from the Latin *rubor*, 'red', the colour of the flowers. The generic name is thought to derive from the Greek *geranos*, 'crane', the long fruit being likened to the beak of the bird.

HOGWEED *see* COW PARSNIP

HOLLY   *Ilex aquifolium*
It is often said that the common name comes from the word 'holy' but there is no evidence to support this. It reaches us

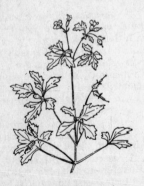

Herb Robert   *Honesty*

from its Anglo-Saxon name *holegn*; Dr Prior (1870) suggests this is derived from the Latin *ulex*, used in very early times for a prickly shrub and which was confused with *ilex*, the early name for the holm oak. This latter name, now used for the genus, is of unknown meaning. The specific *aquifolium* means 'with pointed leaves'.

HOLM OAK *see* EVERGREEN OAK

HONESTY   *Lunaria annua*
The common name has been applied because the fruiting pods are thin and almost transparent, thus revealing the truth of their contents. The generic *Lunaria*, derived from the Latin *luna*, 'the moon', describes the roundish, silvery seed pods. The specific *annua* means 'annual' but the plant is in fact a biennial, so the name would seem to refer to the fact that once the plant is established the flowers can be seen year after year, mainly because of its prolific seed production.

HOP   *Humulus lupulus*
'Hop' is an adaptation of its Low German name *hoppen*; the name came to this country from the Netherlands, along with the plant's cultivation and use in beer making. It could be connected with words meaning 'head'. The generic *Humulus* may be associated with the Latin *humus*, 'ground', for the plant thrives on rich soil although another reason could be that if the plant is not staked it will grow along the surface of the soil. The specific *lupulus*, 'small wolf', echoes an early name 'willow wolf', given because it used its sharp, hook-like stem teeth to climb over willow trees.

HORSE CHESTNUT   *Aesculus hippocastanum*
Castanea (see under Sweet Chestnut) was the name used for a chestnut tree by Virgil and this with the Greek *hippos* meaning 'horse' acounts for both the specific and common names. The association with the horse is taken from an early use of the nuts as a feedstuff and from the horseshoe-like scar remaining after leaf fall. *Aesculus* is an ancient name for a kind of oak with edible fruit, from the Latin *esca*, 'food' or 'nourishment'.

HORSE RADISH   *Armoracia rusticana*
The term 'radish' probably derives from the Latin *radix* meaning 'root', with the prefix 'horse' indicating it is a large coarse kind. *Armoracia*, the generic name, is really of unexplained origin. There is a possibility that it refers to the plant's strong flavour; many plants with powerful tastes were considered 'war plants' and used to build up courage before a battle. The word

Horse chestnut   *Knapweed*

'armour' derives from the Old French *armure*. The specific *rusticana* means 'of the country'.

HORSESHOE VETCH   *Hippocrepis comosa*
The fruits pods are arranged in a horseshoe shape, which accounts for the common and generic names, the latter being derived from the Greek *hippos*, 'horse', and *crepis*, 'shoe'. The plant has vetch-like flowers (see bush vetch). The specific *comosa*, 'bearing a tuft', usually refers to hairs, but in this case seems more descriptive of its tufted habit of growth.

HORSETAIL   *Equisetum arvense*
The slender stems with their whorls of long thin leaves have been likened to the tail of a horse, hence the common name and the generic *Equisetum*, for this derives from the Latin *equus*, 'horse' and *seta*, 'bristle'. The specific *arvense* means 'growing in fields'.

HOUND'S TONGUE   *Cynoglossum officinale*
The common and generic names have the same origins; they refer either to the shape of the leaves resembling a dog's tongue, or to the rough, spiny covering to the fruit which is somewhat tongue-like in texture. The generic name derives from the Greek *kyon*, 'dog', and *glossa*, 'tongue'. The specific *officinale* means 'of the shop'; the plant was much used in early medicine, particularly for skin diseases and dog bites.

HOUSELEEK   *Sempervivum tectorum*
(Welcome-home-husband-however-drunk-you-be)

31

The shorter common name simply means 'house plant', the latter part of the name deriving from the Anglo-Saxon *leac*, 'plant'. It can often be seen growing on roofs and was once often planted there as a protection from witchcraft and lightning. The longer common name probably alludes to the leaning flowering stems, but could also be a further reference to the magical properties of the plant, even a drunk husband being better than none. The generic name derives from the Latin *semper*, 'always', and *vivo*, 'alive', the plant being able to survive under the most arid conditions. This acounts for its being able to grow so well on roof tops, a capacity reflected in the specific *tectorum*, 'of roofs'.

HYACINTH *see* BLUEBELL

IRON-ROOT *see* ORACHE

IVY   *Hedera helix*
The name 'ivy' reaches us from the Anglo-Saxon name *ifig* but what this meant is unknown. The generic *Hedera* is another ancient name whose meaning has been lost. The specific *helix* means 'spiral' or 'twisted', and probably refers to the way the plant twists around the tree trunks on which it often grows. It also has been suggested that the name could have been applied because it is a favourite haunt of snails, called *helix* because of their spiral shells.

IVY-LEAVED TOADFLAX   *Cymbalaria muralis*
The common name indicates that it is a plant with toadflax-like flowers and ivy-shaped leaves. The generic *Cymbalaria* derives from the Greek *kymbalon*, 'cymbal', a reference to the shape of the leaves of some species. The specific *muralis* means 'growing on walls'.

JUNIPER   *Juniperus communis*
The common and generic names are very ancient and of unknown meaning. The specific *communis* can mean 'common' or 'growing in company'; it can be a dominant species in some areas.

KIDNEY VETCH   *Anthyllis vulneraria*
The common name means that it is a plant with vetch-like flowers and kidney-shaped lower leaves; it has also been suggested that its name came from an early medical use in the treatment of various kidney disorders. The generic *Anthyllis* is thought to derive from the Greek *anthos*, 'flower', and *ioulos*, 'down', for the flowers are unusually downy. The specific

vulneraria means 'wound healing', from another early use of this plant.

KINGCUP (Marsh Marigold, May Blobs)   *Caltha palustris*
The name 'kingcup' probably means simply a large, king-sized buttercup-like flower, though it is also said to be because the unopened flower bud is like the gold studs worn by kings (cup being taken from the Anglo-Saxon *copp*, 'head'). These tight buds have also been likened to galls; the Anglo-Saxon *mearge-alla* means 'horse-gall' and hence provides the origin of the name 'marigold'. The prefix 'marsh', used because it is a plant of wet places, is emphasised by the specific *palustris* meaning 'of marshes'. 'May blobs' could derive either from the Anglo-Saxon *mere*, 'marsh', and *blob* or *bleb*, 'bladder', again in reference to the unopened flower buds, or perhaps the name could be associated with the month in which the flowers usually appear. The generic *Caltha* derives from the Greek *kalathos*, 'goblet', from the shape of the flower.

KNAPWEED (Hardheads)   *Centaurea nigra*
Both common names refer to the flower buds, 'knapweed' being probably a corruption of 'knop-' or 'knobweed', and 'hard-heads' alluding to a similarity between this and the weapon of war called a loggerhead, an iron ball on a long handle. The name *Centaurea* honours Chiron the Centaur who used some similar plant to heal wounds in his foot received from an arrow poisoned with the blood of the Hydra. The specific *nigra* means 'black'—the bracts of the flower have a terminal appendage which, in this species, is dark brown or black.

LADY'S MANTLE   *Alchemilla vulgaris*
The common name refers to the shape of the leaves, these being likened to the sleeveless cloaks that ladies used to wear. *Alchemilla* is said to derive from the Arabic *alkemelych*, indicating its use in alchemy. *Vulgaris* is 'common'.

LADY'S SMOCK *see* CUCKOO FLOWER

LADY'S TRESSES   *Spiranthes spiralis*
The generic name derives from the Greek *speira*, 'spiral', and *anthos*, 'flower'; the specific name also means 'spiral'. These and the common name all refer to the shape of the flowering head, the flower spike having the flowers arranged in a roughly twisted row. In the common name this has been likened to braided hair.

LARCH
Larix decidua

The common name is taken from the ancient Latin *Larix* which is now used as a generic name and is of unknown origin. The specific *decidua* means 'deciduous'; the tree is somewhat unusual for a conifer in this respect.

LESSER CELANDINE (Pilewort)
Ranunculus ficaria

The plant is called celandine because it is in flower by the time the swallow (Greek *chelidon*) arrives, and the prefix 'lesser' separates the plant from the greater celandine, a quite unrelated species. The specific *ficaria*, 'fig-like', refers to the small tubers of the plant. These were once used to treat haemorrhoids, hence the name 'pilewort'. The generic name has already been considered (see Creeping Buttercup).

LILY-OF-THE-VALLEY
Convallaria majalis

The term 'lily' is an ancient name that has been used in some Oriental languages as just meaning a 'flower'. The plant is often found on wooded valley sides, hence the common name, and the generic name derives from the Latin *convallium*, 'valley'. The specific *majalis* means 'flowering in May'.

LING *see* HEATHER

LINNAEA
Linnaea borealis

This rare plant is included because it honours the great Swedish classifier Carolus Linnaeus; the name was selected by Dr J. F. Gronovius who gained the permission of Linnaeus to use it because this 'little northern plant, long overlooked, depressed, abject and flowering early' so well illustrated the famous botanist's early career. The specific *borealis* means 'pertaining to the north', a reference to its distribution.

LIME
Tilia x *europaea*

The common name 'lime' is connected with *linde* which in all the Germanic languages means 'pliant' or 'band' and refers to the use of the inner bark in making cordage. The generic *Tilia* is an ancient name of obscure origin; it might derive from the Greek *ptilon*, 'feather', because of the membranous bracteoles (small leaf-like structures) beneath the flowers. The specific *europaea* means 'of Europe'; the prefix 'x' in this name shows it to be of hybrid origin, having probably resulted from the crossing of the large-leaved and small-leaved limes.

LIVELONG *see* ORPINE

Lady's mantle   *Marsh gentian*

LORDS AND LADIES *see* CUCKOO PINT

LOUSEWORT   *Pedicularis sylvatica*
The generic name derives from the Latin *pediculus*, 'louse'; this and the common name were applied because of an early belief that animals who grazed upon it would become full of lice. The pastures where the plant might be found are likely to be very poor and only support weak and unhealthy stock which would account for this belief. The specific *sylvatica* is usually considered to mean 'of woodland' but here means simply 'wild', it is a plant of bogs and heaths rather than woodland.

LUNGWORT   *Pulmonaria officinalis*
The generic name derives from the Latin *pulmo*, 'lung'; this and the common name have been applied because the plant had a great reputation as a cure for lung disorders. Hence, too, the specific *officinalis* meaning 'of the shop'; it would certainly have been found on the premises of the herbalists.

LUPIN   *Lupinus nootkatensis*
The common and generic names derive from the Latin *lupus*, 'wolf', an allusion to an erroneous early belief that the plants had an impoverishing effect upon the soil. The specific *nootkatensis* derives from Nootka Sound, an area in British Columbia where this plant was first found.

MALLOW *see* MARSH MALLOW, MUSK MALLOW

MARJORAM
Origanum vulgare

The common name first belonged to the sweet marjoram (*Marjorana hortensis*) and probably arose as a corruption of its Arabic name *maryamych*. It has been suggested that the name could honour a Greek youth, Amarakos, who was turned into the plant after dropping a vase of scent belonging to the king of Cyprus. The generic *Origanum*, a classical Greek name, might derive from *oros*, 'mountain', and *ganos*, 'brightness' or 'joy', describing a typical place of growth and the pleasant aromatic appearance. The specific *vulgare* means 'common'.

MARSH GENTIAN
Gentiana pneumonanthe

The common and generic name honours Gentius, a king of Illyria, an ancient area of the Adriatic, who first used some of these plants in medicine. The prefix 'marsh' indicates its preference for wet habitats. The specific *pneumonanthe* means 'lung flower'; the plant was once commonly used in treating a number of respiratory diseases.

MARSH MALLOW
Althaea officinalis

The name 'mallow' derives from the Anglo-Saxon *malwe* and Latin *malva* both of which are linked with the Greek *malache*, 'mallow', which is connected with *malakos*, 'soft', because of its emollient medicinal properties. The scientific name also refers to such uses, as the generic name derives from the Greek *althaia*, 'healing medium', and the specific *officinalis* means 'of the shop'. The prefix 'marsh' refers to the plant's liking for marshes near the sea.

MARSH MARIGOLD, MAY BLOBS *see* KINGCUP

MEADOW SAFFRON (Autumn Crocus, Naked Ladies)
Colchicum autumnale

The true saffron (*Crocus sativus*) is sufficiently similar to this plant to explain the first two names. 'Naked ladies' describes the beautiful flower that appears in the autumn with no leaves to hide it; they appear in spring. Hence, too, the specific, 'of autumn'. The generic name derives from Colchis in Asia Minor, where some of these plants were very common.

MEADOW SAXIFRAGE
Saxifraga granulata

The generic *Saxifraga* and the common name 'saxifrage' derive from the Latin *saxum*, 'stone', and *frango*, 'I break', and refer to the use of some species medicinally in clearing 'stones' from the bladder and kidney. Some of these plants inhabit rocky places and were thought to break up the stone on which they lived; this no doubt suggested the medical use. The specific *granulata* means 'granulated' and refers to the bulbils produced in the axils of the lower leaves by means of which the plant overwinters.

MEADOW VETCHLING   *Lathyrus pratensis*
The common name means a small spurious vetch (see Bush Vetch) whilst the specific *pratensis*, 'of meadows', refers to its usual place of growth. The generic *Lathyrus* is an ancient Greek name for some leguminous species.

MEADOWSWEET   *Filipendula ulmaria*
The common name could be a corruption of the Anglo-Saxon *mede-* or *medo-wyrt* meaning 'mead' or 'honey-herb'; the flowers were once added to drinks to impart a sweet, pleasant flavour. The generic name has been considered under 'Dropwort', whilst the specific *ulmaria*, 'elm-like', refers to leaf shape.

MELILOT   *Melilotus officinalis*
The common and generic names derive from the Greek *meli* meaning 'honey', referring to the very sweet scent of the flowers, and *lotos* a very ancient name of unknown meaning, used for these plants by Turner in 1548. The specific *officinalis* shows that the plant was widely used in medicine, especially for poultices.

MIGNONETTE   *Reseda lutea*
The common name derives from the French *mignon*, 'dainty', and is usually applied to the fragrant garden plant (*R. stricta*). The generic *Reseda* is taken from the Latin *resido*, 'calm down', in reference to the medicinal qualities of some of these plants, particularly in applications to bruises. The specific *lutea* means 'yellow', the colour of the flowers.

MILK THISTLE *see* SOW THISTLE

MILKWORT   *Polygala vulgaris*
The generic name derives from the Greek *polys*, 'much', and *gala*, 'milk'. This and the common name could have been applied for a number of reasons: some species have a milky sap, whilst it was an early belief that cattle who grazed upon it would produce abundant milk. Similarly it was thought good for nursing mothers. The specific *vulgaris* means 'common'.

MISTLETOE   *Viscum album*
The common name reaches us from its Anglo-Saxon title

misteltan, but though many fanciful suggestions have been proposed as to reasons for this name its origin remains unknown. The generic *Viscum* is also a very old Latin word used both for the plant and for birdlime. The specific *album*, 'white', refers to the colour of the berries.

MOON DAISY (Ox-eye Daisy)
Chrysanthemum leucanthemum
The common names both indicate a large daisy, comparing the flowers, with their white outer petals and golden centre, to the moon or to an animal's eye. The generic name derives from the Greek *chrysos*, 'gold', and *anthemom*, 'flower', some species having golden flowers. The specific *leucanthemum*, from the Greek *leukos*, 'white', refers to the long, white ray florets.

MOSCHATEL (Townhall Clock, Five-faced Bishop)
Adoxa moschatellina
'Moschatel' and the specific name derive from the Greek *moschos* meaning 'musk', because of a faint smell the plant is reputed to have, especially in damp weather. 'Townhall clock' refers to the shape of the flowering head; it has four flowers facing outwards rather like the clock faces on a tower. A fifth flower faces upwards and accounts for the name 'five-faced bishop'. The generic *Adoxa* derives from the Greek *a*, 'without', and *doxa*, 'glory'—for the small green flowers are so easily missed amongst the green leaves.

MOUSE-EAR HAWKWEED   *Hieracium pilosella*
Some of these plants were said to have been used by hawks to improve their vision; they have also been used in medicines to make one 'see like a hawk'. Hence the common and generic names; the latter is of very ancient origin and derives from the Greek *hierax*, 'hawk'. The specific *pilosella* is taken from the Latin *pilosus*, 'hairy', and refers to the soft, downy leaves whose shape and texture have also been likened to mouse ears.

MULLEIN *see* AARON'S ROD

MUSK MALLOW   *Malva moschata*
The common name refers to the slightly fragrant leaves, as does the specific *moschata*, meaning 'musk'. The name 'mallow' is probably taken from the Latin *Malva*; these have both been considered under 'Marsh Mallow'.

MUSK THISTLE   *Carduus nutans*
The common name refers to its somewhat musky scent and

Mignonette   *Nipplewort*

the strong prickly leaves. 'Thistle' derives from its Anglo-Saxon name *thistel*, which is of unknown meaning. The generic *Carduus* is an old Latin name, also of obscure origin. The specific *nutans* means 'nodding' and refers to the often drooping flower heads.

MUSTARD *see* WHITE MUSTARD

NAVELWORT *see* PENNYWORT

NETTLE *see* STINGING NETTLE

NIGHTSHADE *see* BITTERSWEET, DEADLY NIGHTSHADE

NIPPLEWORT   *Lapsana communis*
The common name is thought to refer to an early medicinal use in the treatment of sore nipples. Medicine also plays a part in the generic name which may derive from the Greek *lapazo* meaning 'I purge'. The specific *communis* means 'common' or 'growing in society'.

OAK (Common or Pedunculate Oak)   *Quercus robur*
The common name derives from the Anglo-Saxon *ac*, 'fruit' or 'acorn', whilst the prefix 'pedunculate', which means 'stalked', refers to the quite long stalks to the acorns. The generic *Quercus* is an old Latin name of obscure origin; it might be associated with the Greek *choiros*, 'pig', because these animals are fond of acorns. The specific name *robur* is usually taken

to mean 'strength' but has also been used as 'hardwood' and 'élite', all terms that are well descriptive of this fine tree.

OLD MAN'S BEARD (Traveller's Joy)   *Clematis vitalba*

'Old man's beard' is a name that has been applied because of the masses of long, white, feathery styles on the fruits. The other often-used name, 'traveller's joy', could refer to the way it adorns the roadsides, to the shelter it can provide or perhaps to its wood, said to be good for making fires. The generic *Clematis* derives from the Greek *klema*, 'vine-branch', refering to the scrambling vine-like habit of growth, and the specific *vitalba* means 'white vine', probably referring to the white flowers and light-coloured, downy sepals.

ORACHE (Iron-root)   *Atriplex patula*

The generic *Atriplex*, an ancient Latin name, could perhaps derive from the Latin *ater*, 'black', in allusion to the colour of the seeds—and to its being worthless as a food. Another possibility lies in an early name 'golden herb', applied because some species were used to treat jaundice, this name being written as *aurago* in Medieval Latin. This could have been corrupted to the French *arroche* from which the common name 'orache' and generic *Atriplex* could derive. The other name 'iron-root' is occasioned by the very strong root system which is very difficult to break or remove. The specific *patula*, 'broad' or 'spreading', refers to the plant's open habit of growth.

ORCHID see BIRD'S-NEST ORCHID, EARLY PURPLE ORCHID

ORPINE (Livelong)   *Sedum telephium*

The name 'orpine' is curious in that it comes from the French *orpiment*, 'yellow pigment', and was used by early writers for some yellow-flowered members of the genus; then in later times the name was quite illogically transferred to almost the only European member with pink flowers! It is called 'livelong' because it remains green some time after being picked. The generic *Sedum* could derive from the Latin *sedere*, 'to sit', from the way many members sit upon walls and roofs. It could also be connected with the Latin *sedare*, 'to calm', in reference to the medicinal qualities of the houseleek, called a *Sedum* in earlier times. The specific *telephium*, an ancient name for the plant, perhaps honours Telephus, a king of Mysia, or Telephus, son of Hercules.

OSIER (Willow) *Salix viminalis*
'Osier' is a French name taken from the medieval Latin *oseria*, from which was derived *oseretum*, 'withy-bed'. The name 'willow' is of unknown meaning though the pliancy of its branches has led to the suggestion that it implies a 'willingness' to be worked in basketry. The generic *Salix* is an old Latin name of unknown meaning, whilst the specific *viminalis*, 'slender', describes the characteristic long, thin, branches.

OX-EYE DAISY *see* MOON DAISY

PARSLEY *Petroselinum crispum*
The generic name derives from the Greek *petros*, 'stone', and *selinon*, 'parsley', many of these plants growing on rocky, stony places; it is an ancient name used by Dioscorides. In time it became *petrosilium* which was anglicised to 'petersylinge' which gradually became 'persele', 'persely' and finally our present common name 'parsley'. The specific *crispum* means 'curled' and refers to the leaves.

PARSNIP *Pastinaca sativa*
The common name is a corruption of its earlier name 'pasnep' which originated in the Latin *pastinaca*, now used as the generic name. This possibly derives from the Latin *pastinum*, 'dibble', the root being likened to this garden tool. The name could alternatively be connected with the Latin *pastus*, 'pasture', as the plant is often found in old grassland. The specific *sativa* means 'cultivated'.

PASQUE FLOWER *Anemone pulsatilla*
The common name was originally written 'passeflower' and was changed to 'pasque' by Gerard in 1597; it refers to the plant's flowering around Passion Week. The generic *Anemone* might derive from the Greek *anemos*, 'wind', some species favouring windy places. Traditionally the flowers opened at the command of the first mild breeze of spring. The specific *pulsatilla* means 'trembling', perhaps applied because, as the flowers appear almost before any other vegetation has started growing, they are devoid of shelter and thus the slightest wind will move the flowering heads.

PEAR *Pyrus communis*
The generic *Pyrus* is an old Classical name of unknown origin. The common name probably also originated in this way reaching us via its French name *poire*. The specific *communis* means 'common' or 'growing in company'.

PENNYROYAL
Mentha pulegium

The common name is a corruption of an early Latin name for the plant, *Puleium regium*; this was written in some herbals as *puliol royal*, words that can be translated 'a sovereign killer of fleas'. This property is also reflected in the specific *pulegium* derived from the Latin *pulex*, 'flea'. The generic *Mentha* honours a Greek nymph, Minthe, daughter of Cocytus, who was turned into a plant of mint by Persephone in a fit of jealousy.

PENNYCRESS
Thlaspi arvense

The common name describes this somewhat cress-like plant with round, flat seed pods which, when ripe, can be likened to silver pennies. The generic *Thlaspi* is an old Greek name for some kind of cress, possibly deriving from the Greek *thlao*, 'I compress', again because of the shape of the fruiting pods. The specific *arvense* means 'growing in fields'. It is a typical weed of arable land in many areas.

PENNYWORT (Navelwort)
Umbilicus rupestris

The common names refer to the shape of the leaves, 'pennywort' because they are rounded and penny-sized and 'navelwort' because of the concave depression in their centre. Hence too the generic *Umbilicus*, from the Latin for 'navel'. The specific *rupestris* means 'rock-loving'. It is a typical plant of many rocky areas and of old stone walls.

PERIWINKLE
Vinca minor

The generic *Vinca* possibly derives from the Latin *vincio*, 'I bind'; the long, pliable stems have been used in the past for tying and binding, especially in the making of wreaths. The specific *minor* means 'lesser' and is used in comparison with the larger, introduced greater periwinkle (*V. major*). The common name probably derives from the Latin name, reaching us via its early English name 'pervinke'.

PIGNUT *see* EARTHNUT

PILEWORT *see* LESSER CELANDINE

PIMPERNEL *see* SCARLET PIMPERNEL

PINE *see* SCOTS PINE

PLOUGHMAN'S SPIKENARD
Inula conyza

The common name uses 'ploughman' as meaning a poor man, whilst the term 'spikenard', a scent obtained from an Indian plant with spiked inflorescence, is applied because this plant has an aromatic root, one which the plough might easily bring up. The generic *Inula* is thought to be a corruption of *Helenium,* an old name for elecampane, a well-known member of the genus. *Helenium* could have been applied in honour of Helen of Troy, either because of the plant's golden flowers or because, traditionally, she had her hands full of its blossoms when Paris stole her away. The specific *conyza* possibly derives from the Greek *konis*, 'dust'; the dried and powdered leaves having been once used to drive off flies and moths.

POPPY *see* FIELD POPPY, WELSH POPPY

PRIMROSE *Primula vulgaris*
The common name reaches us from its early English name, 'primrole' or 'pryme rolles' which are taken from its French name *primevere*, in turn derived from the Latin *primus*, 'first', and *ver*, 'spring', because of its early flowering. It is probable that in translation from the French some confusion was made between *primevere* and *primerose*, French name for the hollyhock which has a much more rose-like flower. The generic name has been considered under Cowslip, and the specific *vulgaris* means 'common'.

PRIVET *Ligustrum vulgare*
The common name comes from the earlier 'primprint' which was taken from the French *prime printemps*, 'first spring'. This was first given to the primrose, a plant that for some reason was called *Ligustrum* in the Latin of the Middle Ages. On the

Pennyroyal

Ploughman's spikenard

43

Continent *Ligustrum* was the name given to privet, derived
from the Latin *ligare*, 'to tie', the flexible branches having been
once used for binding. It was adopted as a generic name by
Turner, so that there being two different species called *Ligustrum*, the name primprint was erroneously given to this plant.
The specific *vulgare* means 'common'.

RAGGED ROBIN
Lychnis flos-cuculi

The common name is probably due simply to its being a red-
flowered plant with deeply divided 'ragged' petals. It has been
suggested that there is an association between the plant and
an early farce once enacted in some country places around the
time of Pentecost, called 'Robin and Marion'. In this the
characters who portrayed the keeper's followers were called,
in the New Forest, Ragged Robins. The generic *Lychnis* derives
from the Greek *lychnos*, 'lamp', probably because of the bril-
liant flower colour in many species. The specific *flos-cuculi*
means 'flower of the cuckoo'; the plant flowers around the
time the cuckoo arrives.

RAGWORT
Senecio jacobaea

The common name probably refers to the deeply divided leaves
whilst *jacobaea* means 'pertaining to James'; in almost all
European languages the plant is dedicated to St. James. It was
said to flower on St. James's Day (25th July); it was used to
cure sores and ulcers once so common amongst pilgrims of
whom the saint was patron; and was also used in treating certain diseases of horses and St. James was their patron also.
The origin of the generic name has been considered previously
under Groundsel.

RAMSONS
Allium ursinum

The common name derives from the Anglo-Saxon *hramsa*,
'rank', describing the strong smell and taste of the plant which
produces unpleasant-tasting milk and butter if eaten by dairy
cows. The generic *Allium* is the classical Latin name for garlic
but its original meaning is unknown. The specific *ursinum*
means 'pertaining to bears' either from an old belief that they
were fond of the plant or perhaps simply meaning a 'strong'
or 'coarse' garlic.

RED BARTSIA
Odontites verna

The common name refers to its being red-flowered, with the
term bartsia (a generic name for a group that used to contain
this species) honouring a Prussian botanist, John Bartsch
(1709-1738). *Odontites* derives from the Greek for tooth, either
in allusion to the four-toothed calyx or to the rather one-sided

Primrose

Red campion

flowering head being likened to a jaw with teeth sticking out. The specific *verna* means 'of spring'; the plant just qualifies for this title by flowering in the late spring.

RED CAMPION   *Silene dioica*
The common name recalls that the red flowers were once used in the chaplets with which the champions of public games were crowned. It is derived from the French *campion*, from the Latin *campus*, 'plain' or 'sports field', where such contests would have been held. The generic *Silene* possibly derives from the Greek *sialon*, 'saliva'; a sticky exudation is found on the stems of many species. The specific *dioica* means 'dioecious', the sexes being carried on separate plants.

RED CLOVER   *Trifolium pratense*
The common name 'clover' which reaches us from the earlier name 'claver' is perhaps associated with its Dutch name *klaver* which may derive from the Latin *clava* meaning 'club', the three-lobed leaves being likened to the three-knotted club of Hercules. Hence, too, the generic name which means 'three-leaved'. The prefix 'red' obviously refers to the colour of the flower whilst the specific *pratense* means 'growing in meadows'.

RESTHARROW   *Ononis repens*
The common name arose in earlier days before farm mechanisation when the plant's strong, matted roots could impede the progress of plough or harrow. The generic *Ononis*, an old Greek name, perhaps derives from *onos*, 'an ass', and *oninemi*,

'I delight'; an old belief was that such animals loved to graze the young shoots and to roll upon the older plants to scratch their backs, some species possessing spines. The specific *repens* means 'creeping'; it creeps through the soil with underground stems (rhizomes).

RIBWORT   *Plantago lanceolata*
The leaves are long and gradually tapering, hence the use of the specific *lanceolata*, 'spear-shaped'. They possess prominent parallel veins which account for the common name 'ribwort'. The generic *Plantago* is thought to derive from the Latin *planta*, 'sole' (of the foot), the leaves of some species such as the greater plantain (*P.major*) being likened to a footprint. Another reason for the name could be because a number of species grow extremely well in firmly trodden areas.

ROCKROSE   *Helianthemum chamæcistus*
The common name refers to its being a brightly coloured, somewhat rose-like flower that often grows amongst rocks. The generic *Helianthemum* also alludes to the bright flowers for it derives from the Greek *helios*, 'sun', and *anthemon*, 'flower'. The specific name means 'dwarf cistus', *cistus* being an old Greek name for a rockrose, perhaps deriving from *kiste*, 'box', in reference to the capsule-like fruit.

ROSE *see* DOG ROSE

ROSEBAY WILLOWHERB (Fireweed)
                                Chamaenerion angustifolium
'Rosebay' is a name that was given to the oleander by Turner and the resemblance in leaf shape between this and the present plant accounts for both the common and generic name; *Chamaenerion* derives from the Greek *chamai,* 'dwarf', and *nerion*, 'oleander'. The specific *angustifolium* means 'narrow-leaved'; their likeness to those of the willow explains the term 'willowherb'. The name 'fireweed' is either used to describe the resemblance of the flowering plants in mass to a blazing fire or, more likely, from its liking for burnt ground. Some people will remember the sudden appearance of the plant in great numbers on the London bomb sites of the Second World War.

SAINFOIN   *Onobrychis viciifolia*
The common names derives from the French *sain*, 'wholesome', and *foin*, 'hay', for it is valuable as forage. This is also reflected in the generic *Onobrychis* which is said to derive from the Greek *onos*, 'ass', and *brycho*, 'I gnaw', or, as is sometimes

said, 'bellow'. The specific *viciifolia* means having 'vetch-like leaves'.

ST. JOHN'S WORT   *Hypericum perforatum*

The leaves possess many glandular dots which look like tiny holes, hence the use of the specific *perforatum* meaning 'pierced'. An old belief tells that these spots ooze blood on 29th August, the day John the Baptist was executed, whilst another idea was that the spots first appear on this day. These beliefs account for the common name. The generic *Hypericum* possibly derives from the Greek *hyper*, 'over', and *eikon*, 'image', from some fancied resemblance between parts of the flower and a human figure or because the flowers were once placed over sacred objects on Walpurgis Night—the plant was held in great repute for its power against witchcraft and evil.

SALAD BURNET   *Poterium sanguisorba*

The plant can be eaten in salads and is very similar to the greater burnet (*Sanguisorba officinalis*) whose dull red flowers account for the name 'burnet', this deriving from the Old French *burnette*, 'brown cloth'. The generic name possibly derives from the Greek *poterion*, 'drinking cup', either from the shape of the calyx or from its early use in cooling drinks. The specific *sanguisorba* is taken from the Latin *sanguis*, 'blood', and *sorbere*, 'to absorb', and again refers to similarities between this and the greater burnet, which was once of great repute for healing wounds and arresting bleeding.

Sainfoin

Sanicle

SANICLE   *Sanicula europaea*
The common and generic names are of uncertain origin, perhaps being associated with the Latin *sanare*, 'to heal'; they could also have arisen by corruption of 'St. Nicholas'. Whatever the derivation, in the Middle Ages the name was synonymous with healing; this is reflected in an old country saying: 'He who keeps sanicle laughs at the doctor.' The specific *europaea* means 'of Europe'.

SAW-WORT   *Serratula tinctoria*
The generic *Serratula* derives from the Latin *serrula*, 'a small saw'; the toothed margin of the leaves accounts for this and for the common name. The specific *tinctoria* means 'of dyers'; in Sweden a yellow dye suitable for colouring woollen cloth has been extracted from the plant.

SAXIFRAGE *see* MEADOW SAXIFRAGE

SCABIOUS *see* DEVIL'S BIT SCABIOUS,
   FIELD SCABIOUS

SCARLET PIMPERNEL (Shepherd's Weatherglass)
                                     Anagallis arvensis
The name 'scarlet pimpernel' is of very uncertain origin; the first part refers to the colour of the flowers but why 'pimpernel'? This name was given to the burnet saxifrage (*Pimpinella saxifraga*) on account of its feathery leaves, but it is a very different plant to this. It is just possible that the name could be connected with the Old French *pimper* meaning 'trim' or 'smart', descriptions that could well be used for this charming little plant. The alternative name, 'shepherd's weatherglass', alludes to the plant's closing its flowers before the onset of rain. The generic *Anagallis* is a very old name possibly derived from the Greek *anagelao*, 'I laugh'; there was an early belief that some of these plants had great powers in removing despondency. The specific *arvensis* means 'growing in fields'.

SCOTS PINE   *Pinus sylvestris*
This tree's dominance in wide areas of the Scottish Highlands explains part of the common name. The term 'pine' is taken from the Latin *Pinus*, now used as the generic name. This word is of very obscure origin; it could be a contraction of the Latin *picinus* meaning 'pitchy', or taken from the Sanskrit *pina*, 'fat', because of the tree's rich, resinous secretions. Another possibility is that it is connected with the Greek *pinos*, 'raft', the timber having served for this purpose since very primitive

Shepherd's purse   *Scarlet pimpernel*

times and it was held sacred to the Greek sea god. The specific *sylvestris* means 'growing in woods'.

SEA HOLLY   *Eryngium maritimum*

This is a seashore plant with somewhat holly-like leaves, hence the common name and the use of the specific *maritimum* meaning 'of the coast'. The generic *Eryngium* is taken from the Greek name for some sort of thistle and is said to derive from *ereugomai*, 'I belch', the plant having been once used to relieve flatulence.

SEA LAVENDER   *Limonium vulgare*

Similarities in general appearance between this seashore plant and the true lavender, whose name derives from the Latin *lavare*, 'to wash', from its having been used in soaps and laundry processes, account for its common name. The generic *Limonium* is taken from the Greek *limne*, 'marsh'; it is a typical plant of salt marshes. The specific *vulgaris* means 'common'.

SELF-HEAL   *Prunella vulgaris*

The common name springs from early medicinal uses when the plant was esteemed as a wound herb. The generic *Prunella* is taken from the German *brunella*, which derives from the German *bräune*, 'quinsy', a disease the plant was used to cure. It has also been suggested that the name could be connected with the German *braun*, 'brown', in reference to the colour of the seeding heads. The specific *vulgaris* means 'common'.

SHEEP'S BIT *Jasione montana*

The common name has probably been applied because of similarities between the flowers and those of devil's bit scabious, combined with the fact that the sheep's bit prefers drier ground and is thus often found on areas grazed by sheep. All that is known about the generic *Jasione* is that it was used by Theophrastus and is a Greek name for some wild pot-herb. The specific *montana* means 'of mountains', but the plant is also found in many lowland grassy areas.

SHEPHERD'S NEEDLE *Scandix pecten-veneris*

The common name refers to the long needle-like fruits, as does the specific *pecten-veneris* or 'comb of Venus'. The generic *Scandix* is an ancient Greek name for some eatable plant, no doubt given to this species because it has been eaten by poor people as a very low quality vegetable.

SHEPHERD'S PURSE *Capsella bursa-pastoris*

The specific name derives from the Latin *bursa*, 'purse', and *pastor*, 'shepherd', a description of the little heart-shaped, purse-like fruiting capsules. Hence, too, the common name and even the generic *Capsella* for this derives from the Latin *capsula* meaning a 'small box'.

SILVER BIRCH *Betula pendula*

In the common name the first part refers to the beautiful silvery colour of the bark. The origins of the word 'birch' are complicated; it is similar to words in many European languages meaning 'bark' and perhaps indicated a tree whose bark was used for writing upon, as it was before the invention of paper. The meaning of the generic *Betula* is unknown, whilst the specific *pendula*, 'hanging', describes either the drooping habit of the branches or the male catkins which usually hang in groups of three.

SILVERWEED *Potentilla anserina*

The common name probably refers to the silky, silvery appearance of the leaves, especially the undersides, though another reason could be the little silver-like drops of water often found clinging to the leaf hairs. The generic *Potentilla* derives from the Latin *potens*, 'powerful'; it was an esteemed medicinal herb being used in treating wounds, bruises and fevers. The specific *anserina* means 'pertaining to geese', which readily eat the leaves.

SLOE *see* **BLACKTHORN**

SNAPDRAGON   *Antirrhinum majus*
The generic names derives from the Greek *anti*, 'similar', and
rhis, 'snout', the shape of the flowers being likened to an animal's nose and mouth; the flowers can be made to open by
squeezing the sides—and hence also the common name. The
specific *majus* meaning 'greater' is used in comparison with the
smaller weasel's snout (*A.orontium*) whose flower is about one-
third of the size.

SNOWDROP   *Galanthus nivalis*
The common name refers to the colour and drop-like form of
the flowers, similar to the pendants worn by the ladies of the
sixteenth and seventeenth centuries. The generic *Galanthus*
derives from the Greek *gala*, 'milk', and *anthos*, 'flower', and
the specific *nivalis* means 'snow-white', or 'growing near snow'.

SOLOMON'S SEAL   *Polygonatum multiflorum*
The common name is usually thought to have been applied
because the flat, round scars on the root or the marks that can
be sometimes seen when the root is cut across have been
likened to a six-pointed star called a 'Solomon's seal' by the
Arabs. (The star is formed by two intersecting equilateral
triangles.) The generic *Polygonatum* derives from the Greek
polys, 'many', and *gony*, 'knee', and refers either to the many
knots on the roots or to the much-jointed stem. The specific
multiflorum means 'many-flowered'; in this plant the flowers
are usually carried in groups of five, whilst in other species
the flower groups are of a smaller number.

Solomon's seal   *Spindle*

SOWBREAD
Cyclamen hederifolium

The common name has apparently been applied because in places where the plant is frequent pigs root out and eat the tubers. The generic *Cyclamen* is an old name perhaps deriving from the Greek *kyklos*, 'circle', either because of the coiled seed vessels or from the rounded leaves of some species. In this case the specific *hederifolium* means 'ivy-leaved'.

SOW THISTLE (Milk Thistle)
Sonchus oleraceus

The term 'thistle' has been considered under Carline Thistle whilst the prefix 'sow' probably refers to an early belief that farrowing sows eat the plant in order to increase their milk supply. This could have been suggested by the copious supply of latex in the plant, and also explains the name 'milk thistle'. The generic *Sonchus* is Greek, possibly from *somphos*, 'hollow', referring to the stem structure. The specific *oleraceus* means an 'eatable garden herb'; in the past it was sometimes eaten as a winter salad.

SPANISH CHESTNUT *see* SWEET CHESTNUT

SPINDLE
Euonymus europaeus

The common name refers to an early use of the wood in making skewers and spindles; it derives from the Anglo-Saxon *spinel* meaning 'pin'. The generic *Euonymus* could derive from the Greek *eu*, 'good', and *onoma*, 'name', applied ironically, for the plant is poisonous. It could also simply honour Euonyme, mother of the three Furies of mythology. The specific *europaeus* means 'of Europe'.

SPURGE *see* SUN SPURGE

SPURGE LAUREL
Daphne laureola

The common name refers to the rather laurel-like leaves, as does the specific *laureola* meaning 'little laurel', and links them with spurge (*Euphorbia*) which the plant vaguely resembles and both of which were used medicinally as quite violent purgatives. The generic *Daphne* was once the Greek name for the true laurel (*Laurus nobilis*) and again refers to similarities in leaf shape. It has been suggested that the name derives from the Greek *daio*, 'I burn', and *phone*, 'noise', referring to the loud crackling noise the leaves make when thrown upon a fire. In mythology Daphne was the name of a nymph who was turned into the laurel when being pursued by Apollo.

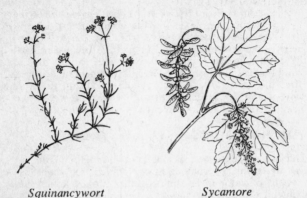

Squinancywort　　　　　　*Sycamore*

SPURREY　　　　　　　　　　*Spergula arvensis*
The origins of the common and generic names are thought to
be the same, perhaps deriving from the Latin *spargo*, 'I scatter',
showing how the fruiting capsules split and widely scatter the
tiny seeds. The specific *arvensis* means 'growing in fields'.

SQUINANCYWORT　　　　　　*Asperula cynanchica*
The specific *cynanchica* means 'dog-throttle' and was the Greek
name for quinsy, a disease the plant was reputed to cure. This
use also explains the common name, for it comes from the
medieval Latin for quinsy, *squinancia*. The generic *Asperula*
derives from the Latin *asper* meaning 'rough', a description of
the texture of the leaves and stems of many species.

STAR THISTLE　　　　　　　*Centaurea calcitrapa*
The common name has been applied because of the prickly,
star-like flowering head. This also accounts for the specific
calcitrapa which derives from the medieval Latin *calx*, 'heel',
and *trappa*, 'snare', which give the name 'caltrop', a four-spiked
iron ball used to impede and maim cavalry horses. The generic
Centaurea has been considered previously under Knapweed.

STEMLESS THISTLE　　　　　　*Cirsium acaulon*
The flower appears to arise straight from the leaf rosettes without any stalk, which accounts for the common name and the
specific *acaulon*, 'stemless'. The term 'thistle' has been discussed
under Carline Thistle. The generic *Cirsium* is said to be derived
from the Greek *kirsos*, 'swollen vein', an affliction which some
of these plants were reputed to cure.

STINGING NETTLE *Urtica dioica*

Everyone knows why this plant has been given the term 'stinging' in its common name but the origins of 'nettle' are much more obscure. It could derive from the Anglo-Saxon *noedl*, 'needle', because of the stings or perhaps because in early days the plant supplied a coarse thread; with careful dressing this could be made almost as fine as silk. The generic *Urtica* derives from the Latin *uro*, 'I burn', another allusion to its stinging powers, and the specific *dioica*, 'dioecious', refers to the sexes being carried on separate plants.

STITCHWORT (Adder's Meat, Satin Flower)
Stellaria holostea

The name 'stitchwort' has been applied either from its early use in curing internal cramp or 'stitch', or from its being thought of value in knitting together broken bones. This also explains the specific *holostea*, 'whole bone'. 'Adder's meat' probably means it was found in areas that snakes were thought to inhabit. The name 'satin flower', which more properly belongs to the honesty, is probably given because of the texture of the white petals. The generic *Stellaria* derives from the Latin *stella*, 'star', the shape of the flowers.

STRAWBERRY *Fragaria vesca*

The common name probably originated from the straw-like runners, though it may be associated with an early custom of selling the fruits threaded upon a grass straw. It has also been suggested that it was given from the practice of placing straw around the plants when grown in the garden. The generic *Fragaria* is thought to derive from the Latin *fragrans*, 'fragrant', from the smell. The specific *vesca* means 'little' or 'weak', no doubt comparing its small fruits with the large ones of garden species.

SUCCORY *see* CHICORY

SUN SPURGE *Euphorbia helioscopia*

The specific name means 'sun follower'—because the stem turns to face the sun; hence also the common name, with 'spurge' referring to its powerful purgative property. The generic *Euphorbia* honours Euphorbus, a physician to Juba, king of Mauritania.

SUNDEW *Drosera rotundifolia*

The common name is thought to be a mis-spelling of the Saxon *sin-dew*, 'always dewy', and no matter how hot the sun shines the plant still retains its dew-covered appearance. The generic *Drosera* also refers to this, being taken from the Greek *droseros*, 'dewy'. The specific *rotundifolia* means round-leaved.

SWEET CHESTNUT (Spanish Chestnut)   *Castanea sativa*
The prefixes 'sweet' and 'Spanish' in the common name refer to the edible fruit; those of the highest quality sold in the London markets were imported from Spain where the trees were grown, hence the specific *sativa* which means 'cultivated'. The generic *Castanea* is the name of a town in Thessaly, Greece, where the plant was first noted. The Greek name was *kastanea* which gave the Latin *castanea*, the Old French *chastaine* and the Middle English *chestaine*, which in turn produced 'chesten nut' and finally 'chestnut'.

SWEET VIOLET   *Viola odorata*
The common name is taken from the Latin *Viola*, now used as a generic name. This was used by the old writers for many sweet-scented flowers but is of unknown meaning other than that it is thought to derive from the same source as the Greek name for 'violet', *ion*. The specific *odorata* means 'sweet-scented'.

SWEET WOODRUFF   *Galium odoratum*
The plant has a pleasant smell, rather reminiscent of new-mown hay, hence the use of the prefix 'sweet' and the specific *odoratum*, 'fragrant'. The herb was once popular for strewing upon floors and hanging in churches and linen cupboards. The name 'woodruff' comes from its Anglo-Saxon name *wude-rofe*; the first part of this means 'wood', a typical place of growth, whilst it is suggested that the term *rofe* is derived from the French *roue*, 'wheel', because of the spoke-like way the leaves are arranged upon the stems. The generic name *Galium* has been considered under Cleavers.

SYCAMORE   *Acer pseudoplatanus*
The common name 'sycamore' originally belonged to the fig, deriving from the Greek *sykon*, 'fig', and was erroneously transferred to this tree by Ruellius. Perhaps he was aided in this, because in the sacred dramas of the Middle Ages the sycamore often provided the foliage that was used to represent the fig in which Mary and her infant Jesus hid from Herod. The generic *Acer* means 'sharp', this being the Latin name for the maple, whose wood served the Romans for spear and javelin shafts. The specific *pseudoplatanus*, 'false plane-tree', is owed to similarities in leaf shape between this plant and the true plane. In North America the name sycamore is always used for the plane.

TEASEL
Dipsacus fullonum

The name 'teasel' derives from the Anglo-Saxon *taesan*, 'to tease', for the dry fruiting heads were used for scratching cloth. This is reflected in the specific *fullonum*, 'of fullers', the heads being used by fullers to comb and raise the nap on cloth. The generic *Dipsacus* derives from the Greek *dipsa*, 'thirst', a reference to the way the leaves clasp the stem and form a hollow that will collect and hold rainwater.

THISTLE *see* CARLINE THISTLE, MUSK THISTLE, STAR THISTLE, STEMLESS THISTLE

THORN APPLE
Datura stramonium

The common name refers to the large spine-covered fruit that can be about the size of a medium apple. The generic *Datura* could be either a vernacular East Indian name for the plant or from its Arabic name, *tatorah*, but what this signified is unknown. The specific *stramonium* is an old medical name for this poisonous plant, but again its meaning is unknown.

THYME
Thymus drucei

The common name is taken from the Latin *Thymus*, now used as the generic name. It is originally ancient Greek, used by Theophrastus, and of obscure meaning, perhaps being connected with the Greek *thymos*, 'courage', in allusion to the stimulating smell, or with *thyos*, 'incense'. The specific *drucei* honours G. C. Druce (1850–1932), a well known botanist, author of the *British Plant List*, a *Comital Flora of the British Isles* and many other works.

TOADFLAX
Linaria vulgaris

The leaves have been likened to those of flax, which accounts for part of the common name, but why the prefix 'toad' has been applied is uncertain. It seems probable that it arose from an early translation error—Dodoens described the plant as '*Herba asimilis cum bubonio facultatis*', meaning that the plant was used to treat hot swellings called 'buboes' and was therefore given the name *bubonium*. In translation this name could have been mistaken for *bufonium* which derives from the Latin *bufo*, 'toad'. Other suggestions for the name are that it simply means a spurious flax, or that toads like to shelter beneath its leaves. The generic *Linaria* derives from the Latin *linum*, 'flax', because of the similarity in leaves mentioned earlier. The specific *vulgaris* means 'common'. See also Ivy-leaved Toadflax.

TOOTHWORT *Lathraea squamaria*
The common name alludes to the somewhat tooth-like scales
that are found on the rootstock and stem base; so also does the
specific *squamaria* meaning 'having small, scale-like leaves'.
The generic *Lathraea* probably derives from the Greek *lath-
raios*, 'concealed', as this parasitic plant is often found in dark,
shaded places, especially under hazel trees.

TOUCH-ME-NOT *Impatiens noli-tangere*
All the names refer to the fact that if the ripe seed-pods are
touched they burst quite violently, scattering their seeds. The
generic *Impatiens* is the Latin word meaning 'hasty' or 'im-
patient' and the specific *noli-tangere* means 'do not touch'.

TRAVELLER'S JOY *see* **OLD MAN'S BEARD**

TULIP *Tulipa sylvestris*
The common and generic names are thought to have arisen by
corruption of the Persian name for the plants, *thoulyban*,
toliban or *tulipant*, which signify 'turban', the shape of the
flower being thought to resemble this oriental head-dress. The
specific *sylvestris* in this case means 'wild'; it can also be used
to mean 'of woodland'.

VALERIAN *Valeriana officinalis*
The common, generic and specific *officinalis* all refer to early
medicinal uses of the plant; it was thought of particular value
in treating cases of hysteria and epilepsy. The generic *Valeriana*
and the common name probably derive from the Latin *valere*
'to be healthy' though it has been said to honour Valerius, a
Roman doctor reputed to have been the first to use the plant
in medicine.

VERVAIN *Verbena officinalis*
The common name is take from the Latin *Verbena,* now used
as the generic name. This is of very obscure origin, perhaps
associated with the Latin *verbenae*, the sacred boughs of olive,
laurel and myrtle once carried in various processions. The plant
has many magical properties ascribed to it, one of which was
being able to reconcile enemies, and ambassadors on errands
of peace would solemnly carry a sprig before them. The specific
officinalis shows that the plant would have been found on the
premises of herbalists, for besides being reputed to cure many
diseases it also offered protection from witchcraft and other
evils.

VETCH see BUSH VETCH, HORSESHOE VETCH, KIDNEY VETCH

VETCHLING see MEADOW VETCHLING

VIOLET see SWEET VIOLET

VIPER'S BUGLOSS — *Echium vulgare*

The generic *Echium* is thought to derive from the Greek *echis*, 'a viper', either from an early use in treating snake bite or because the seeds were fancied to resemble a serpent's head. The name bugloss derives from the Greek *bous*, 'ox', and *glossa*, 'tongue', a description of the shape and texture of the leaves. The specific *vulgare* means 'common'.

WALL-PEPPER — *Sedum acre*

The common name refers to a typical place of growth on old walls and to its biting, acrid taste. Similarly, the specific *acre* means 'sharp' or 'pungent'. The generic *Sedum* has been discussed previously under Orpine.

WALLFLOWER — *Cheiranthus cheiri*

The common name has been applied because it was first introduced from Spain for growing upon walls. The origins of the generic name are obscure; it could be associated with the Greek *cheir*, 'hand', and *anthos*, 'flower', because of their use in sweet-scented bouquets. Another possibility is that it is linked with the Arabic *keiri* or *kheyrey*, the name for some sweet-smelling plant known to the Moors. The specific name has the same origins as the generic title.

WALNUT — *Juglans regia*

The common name comes from the Anglo-Saxon *wealh-hnut*, where *wealh* means 'foreign'; the tree was introduced into northern Europe from Italy. The generic *Juglans* derives from the Latin *Jovis*, 'of Jupiter', and *glans*, 'nut'. Mythology tells how the Greeks dedicated the tree to Diana and held her feasts beneath it; the Romans strewed the nuts at weddings to ensure fertility. The specific *regia* means 'regal', a reference to its majestic stature, to its use in medicine or to its power in combating evil spirits.

WATER-LILY see YELLOW WATER-LILY

WELSH POPPY — *Meconopsis cambrica*

This plant is a true native of Wales and a few areas of southwest England, though it has been widely introduced elsewhere. The common name and the specific *cambrica*, 'of Wales', refer to this. The generic name derives from the Greek *mekon*, 'poppy', and *opsis*, 'like', and refers to the yellow poppy-like flowers.

WHITE BRYONY (Red Bryony)   *Bryonia dioica*
The generic *Bryonia* is thought to derive from the Greek *bryo*, 'I sprout', alluding to the rapid spring growth of the stems. The common name is taken from this very old Latin name, the prefix 'white' referring to the paler colour of the leaves and root as compared with those of black bryony. The other prefix 'red' alludes to the colour of the ripe berries. The specific *dioica* means 'dioecious', the male flowers being on one plant and the female ones on another.

WHITE DEADNETTLE   *Lamium album*
The common name shows it to be a nettle-like plant, with white flowers, that does not sting. The specific *album* meaning 'white', also refers to the flower colour whilst the generic *Lamium*, an old Latin name, perhaps derives from the Greek *laimos*, 'throat', describing the shape of the flowers with their constricted neck.

WHITE MUSTARD   *Sinapis alba*
The name 'mustard' is of very ancient origin and derives from the Old French name *mostarde*. It has been suggested that the name is connected with *mustum*, a Latin word for the juice resulting from the first pressing of grapes which was mixed with the powdered seeds of the plant to produce 'mustard' sauce. The prefix 'white' in the common name and the specific *alba* refer to the seeds, which are a very pale yellow. The meaning of the generic *Sinapis* is unknown.

WHORTLEBERRY *see* BILBERRY

WILLOW *see* OSIER

WILLOWHERB *see* CODLINS AND CREAM, ROSEBAY WILLOWHERB

WOAD   *Isatis tinctoria*
The origin of the common name is uncertain but there is an Anglo-Saxon word, *woed*, which means 'weed' and could be used in the sense of a garment, as in a widow's weeds. The plant was much used as a source of dye for colouring the cloth (as well as the bodies) of our ancestors. This also explains the use

of the specific *tinctoria*, 'of dyers'. The generic *Isatis* is an ancient classical Greek name for some healing herb; it has been suggested that it derives from the Greek *isazo*, 'I make equal', because of a medicinal use in removing roughness from the skin.

WOOD ANEMONE   *Anemone nemorosa*
The origins of the common and generic name 'anemone' have been considered previously under Pasque Flower. The prefix 'wood' refers to its preference for woodland habitats, as does the specific *nemorosa* meaning 'well wooded'.

WOODRUFF *see* SWEET WOODRUFF

WOOD SORREL   *Oxalis acetosella*
The common name indicates that it is a woodland plant with an acid taste, for the term 'sorrel' derives from its French name *surelle*, which itself is a diminutive of the Low German *suur* meaning 'sour'. This also explains the scientific name, for *Oxalis* is from the Greek *oxys*, 'acid', and the specific *acetosella* is from the Latin *acetum*, 'sour'.

WOODY NIGHTSHADE *see* BITTERSWEET

YARROW   *Achillea millefolium*
The common name 'yarrow' is taken from the Anglo-Saxon *gearwe* which appears to have first belonged to the vervain when it signified 'holy'. Perhaps this was applied because of the fame of the plant as a wound herb, a use which is reflected in the generic name. *Achillea* honours the Greek hero Achilles who is said to have used the plant to cure the wounds received by Telephus, son of Hercules. The specific *millefolium* means 'thousand-leaved', a reference to the finely divided foliage.

YELLOW BIRD'S NEST   *Monotropa hypopithys*
The common name has been said to be in contrast to the wild carrot which has been called 'birdsnest' in the past. However the comparison would seem more likely to be with the somewhat similar bird's nest orchid. The prefix 'yellow' refers to the pale, yellowish, waxy appearance of the plant. The generic *Monotropa* derives from the Greek *monos*, 'single', and *tropos*, 'turn', and refers to the way the flowering spike bends and droops to one side. The specific *hypopithys* is of very ancient origin deriving from the Greek *hypo*, 'under', and perhaps from

pitta meaning 'pitch', the latter being a reference to the smell of pines. The plant is often found in pine woods.

YELLOW FLAG   *Iris pseudacorus*

The common name refers to the colour of the flowers and the way the petals quickly go limp and hang loosely from the flowering spike, from the Middle English *flakken* meaning 'to flap'. The generic *Iris* is a Latin word for 'rainbow' and apparently refers to the many and varied colours of the flowers. The specific *pseudacorus* means 'false *Acorus* (sweet flag)'; this present species has many similarities with the true *Acorus*.

YELLOW RATTLE   *Rhinanthus minor*

As the common name says, this is a yellow-flowered plant and when the seeds in the pods are ripe and dry they rattle when the wind shakes the heads. The generic *Rhinanthus* derives from the Greek *rhin*, 'snout', and *anthos*, 'flower', a description of the shape of the flower. The specific *minor*, 'smaller', differentiates this from the much less common greater yellow rattle (*R. major*), a larger plant in all respects.

YELLOW WATER-LILY (Brandy Bottle)   *Nuphar lutea*

This is a yellow-flowered plant of lakes and ponds, which explains the specific *lutea*, which means 'yellow'. The term 'lily', a very ancient word, is of unknown meaning and is used simply as descriptive of a 'pretty flower'. The other common name 'brandy bottle' is from the bottle-shaped fruiting capsule and the rather alcoholic scent sometimes apparent from the flowers. The generic *Nuphar* is thought to derive from *naufar* or *nyloou-*

Yellow flag

Yew

far, the Arabic names for *nymphaea* which is taken from the Greek *nymphe*, 'bride', and used for mythological maidens, such as water nymphs: it is an allusion to the aquatic habitat of these plants.

YEW
Taxus baccata

The common name 'yew' comes from the Anglo-Saxon name *iw* but what this very ancient name originally signified is unknown. The origin of the generic *Taxus* is also very uncertain but is often thought to derive from the Greek *toxon*, 'bow', because of the famous traditional use of the wood. It has also been suggested that the name could derive from the Greek *taxis*, 'arrangement', in reference to the orderly way the leaflets are laid out, rather like the teeth of a comb. The specific *baccata*, 'berried', is another very old word, referring to the bright red fruits.

GLOSSARY

Annual: a plant that completes its life cycle, from seed to flower, within one year.

Biennial: a plant that completes its life cycle in two years, flowering in the second year.

Calyx: the group of sepals as a whole, these being the outer parts of the flower that, in the bud stage, enclose and protect it.

Columella: Roman writer on agriculture who lived about the first century AD.

Dioscorides: Roman physician and writer who lived about AD 40. Compiled a work known as *De materia medica libra quinque* which describes some 500 plants. No contemporary version survives but a Byzantine copy, dated AD 512, does.

Dodoens: born in Malines, 1517, and became the first Belgian botanist of wide repute. The author of a herbal first published in Flemish in 1554. Died 1585.

Family: a group used in classifying plants consisting of a number of similar genera (plural of genus).

Fuchs: born in Bavaria, 1501. Physician, botanist and writer, produced a famous Latin herbal in 1542 describing around 500 species, *De histria stirpium*. Died 1566.

Genus: a group used in classifying plants, usually consisting of a number of similar species. The term 'generic name' is the name given to the genus.

Gerard: 1545–1607; famous as the author of *The Herbal and General History of Plants* which appeared in 1597. A second edition, enlarged and amended by Thomas Johnson, was produced in 1633.

Habitat: a natural place of growth.

Inflorescence: the flowering shoot as a whole.

Linnaeus: 1707–1778; Swedish natural historian, famous for creating a workable classification system from the chaos of earlier workers.

Lyte: born around 1529. Made an English translation of Dodoens' herbal, published in 1578 under the title *A nievve herball, or historie of plantes.*

Perennial: a plant that lives for more than two years, usually flowering each year.

Pliny: AD 23–79. Contemporary of Dioscorides, Roman writer and philosopher. Named Gaius Plinius Secundus, but usually known as Pliny the Elder.

Receptacle: the top of the flower stalk from which the flower parts arise.

Rhizome: an underground stem that persists for more than one year.

Ruellius: 1474–1537. A French physician and botanist famous for his Latin translation of Dioscorides produced in 1516.

Species: the smallest unit of classification *commonly used*. The term 'specific name' is the name given to the species.

Stolon: a surface creeping stem that roots at the nodes (where leaves arise). Hence *stoloniferous*, producing stolons.

Theophrastus: born around 370 BC. Pupil and successor to Aristotle. Famous for an *Enquiry into Plants* which is thought to have been compiled by scholars attending his lectures. Contains the first writings to show any appreciation of ecology.

Turner: born in Morpeth around 1512. Published many works which earned him the title the 'Father of English Botany'.

Virgil: 70–19 BC. Famous Roman poet.

Some titles available in the 'Discovering' series

Abbeys and Priories (25p)
American Story in England (25p)
Antique Firearms (25p)
Antique Maps (30p)
Archaeology in Denmark (40p)
Archaeology in England and Wales (30p)
Artillery (30p)
Banknotes (30p)
Bath Road (25p)
Bells and Bellringing (25p)
Berkshire (20p)
Bird Watching (30p)
Birmingham Road (25p)
Brasses and Brassrubbing (25p)
Bridges (25p)
British Cavalry Regiments (30p)
British Military Badges and Buttons (30p)
British Military Uniforms (30p)
British Postage Stamps (30p)
Bucks Explorer (20p)
Burford (20p)
Castle Combe (15p)
Cathedrals (30p)
Caves (30p)
Chesham (20p)
Cheshire (30p)
Christian Names (30p)
Christmas Customs and Folklore (30p)
Churches (30p)
Church Furniture (25p)
Civic Heraldry (25p)
Comics (30p)
Derbyshire/Peak District (30p)
Devon (20p)
Dorset (30p)
Ecology (30p)
Edged Weapons (30p)
Embroidery in 19th Century (30p)
England's Trees (30p)
English Civil Wargaming (30p)
English County Regiments (25p)
English Customs and Traditions (30p)
English Furniture 1500-1720 (25p)
English Furniture 1720-1830 (30p)
Epitaphs (30p)
Essex (30p)
Exeter Road (25p)
Famous Battles: Marlborough's
  Campaigns (30p)
Famous Battles: Peninsular War (30p)
Flower Arrangement (30p)
Folklore in Industry (25p)
Folklore of Birds and Beasts (30p)
Folklore of Plants (30p)
Footsteps through London's Past (30p)
Forests of Central England (30p)
Gardening for the Handicapped (30p)
Ghosts (30p)
Gloucester Road (25p)
Gloucestershire/Cotswolds (30p)
Hallmarks on English Silver (25p)
Hampshire (25p)
Harness and Saddlery (30p)
Herbs (30p)
Hertfordshire (25p)
High Wycombe (20p)

Highwaymen (25p)
Hill Figures (25p)
Horse Brasses (25p)
Inn Signs (25p)
Investing Your Money (30p)
Kings and Queens (30p)
Leicestershire/Rutland (30p)
Life-boats (30p)
Lincolnshire (30p)
Local History (30p)
London for Children (30p)
London – Statues and Monuments (25p)
Mermaids and Sea Monsters (20p)
Militaria (30p)
Military Traditions (30p)
Modelling for Wargamers (30p)
Model Soldiers (30p)
Narrow Gauge Railways (30p)
Norfolk (20p)
Northamptonshire (25p)
Off-beat Walks in London (30p)
Oil Lamps (30p)
Old Buses and Trolleybuses (30p)
Old Motorcycles (30p)
Oxfordshire (20p)
Period Gardens (30p)
Picture Postcards (25p)
Playing-Cards and Tarots (30p)
Railwayana (30p)
Rules for Wargaming (40p)
Schools (25p)
Sea Shells (30p)
Ship Models (30p)
Somerset (30p)
Space (30p)
Spas (30p)
Staffordshire Figures (30p)
Stained Glass (25p)
Stately Homes (30p)
Statues in C. and N. England (25p)
Statues in S. England (25p)
Suffolk (30p)
Surnames (30p)
Surrey (20p)
Sussex (30p)
This Old House (25p)
Topiary (25p)
Towns (25p)
Toys and Toy Museums (30p)
Traction Engines (25p)
Trade Tokens (25p)
Victorian and Edwardian Furniture (30p)
Walks in the Chilterns (30p)
Wall Paintings (30p)
Wargames (25p)
Warwickshire (30p)
Watermills (25p)
The Westward Stage (45p)
Wild Plant Names (30p)
Wiltshire (30p)
Windsor (25p)
Worcestershire/Herefordshire (30p)
Wrought Iron (25p)
Yorkshire – Moors and Coast (25p)
Yorkshire – West Riding (30p)
Your Family Tree (30p)

Printed in England by Maund & Irvine Ltd., Tring, Herts.